Owen Strachan's excellent work on the development of twentieth-century "classical evangelicalism" is illuminating and even inspirational. It also is realistic about the barriers that can block our best intentions. But in the end I was impressed that we don't have the same godly ambition today as leaders such as Harold John Ockenga, Carl Henry, Billy Graham, and (in the UK) John Stott. The account is convicting and motivating.

—TIM KELLER, Senior Pastor, Redeemer
Presbyterian Church, New York City

Owen Strachan provides an admirable account of one of the most important developments in twentieth-century American evangelical thought. Beginning in the 1940s, Harold Ockenga, pastor of Park Street Church in Boston, mobilized mostly younger evangelical scholars to form a self-conscious intellectual community. The ensuing renewal of evangelical intellectual life provided an important dimension for the new evangelical movement associated with Billy Graham and continues to have significant effects through the institutions shaped by that generation. Strachan introduces new material for telling this story and tells the story well.

—GEORGE MARSDEN, Emeritus Professor of History,
Notre Dame University

Studded with rich insights, *Awakening the Evangelical Mind* is a page-turning book that chronicles the efforts of Harold Ockenga, Carl F. H. Henry, Kenneth S. Kantzer, Billy Graham, and others to reinvigorate the "evangelical mind" after World War II. Author Owen Strachan helps his readers to sense the joys and poignant disappointments of these men as they pursued their important campaign. Based on previously unexploited archives, this is a study no student of the American evangelical movement can afford to miss.

—JOHN WOODBRIDGE, Research Professor of History,
Trinity Evangelical Divinity School

Owen Strachan locates the birth of neo-evangelicalism in an improbable place: along the banks of the Charles River, in Harvard's hallowed halls and Boston's venerable Park Street Church. There, during the era of World War II, a formidable group of "Boston scholars" dreamed of fashioning an intellectually powerful movement that could help reach

America for Christ. Anyone wanting to understand the continuing strength of evangelical faith in America should read this fascinating book.

—Thomas Kidd, Professor of History,
Baylor University

Owen Strachan has given us a remarkable account of the neo-evangelical movement and the formation of evangelical scholarship as it developed in the middle of the twentieth century. Strachan's brilliantly researched and carefully written work offers us much more than a recounting of this important movement. Through the eyes of Harold Ockenga, Carl Henry, E. J. Carnell, and others, *Awakening the Evangelical Mind* provides us with fresh insights into the shaping of relationships, the formation—and attempted formation—of important institutions, and an even-handed analysis of the accomplishments and setbacks of those who were at the center of these most significant days in the history of the American evangelical movement. We salute Owen Strachan for this masterful contribution!

—David S. Dockery, President,
Trinity International University

In this well-researched and beautifully crafted book, Owen Strachan introduces us to a remarkable group of mid-twentieth-century evangelicals whose passion for recovering the life of the mind helped to reshape the modern evangelical movement. Rather than abandoning the academy, as some had done in the immediate past, they enthusiastically embraced it and inspired growing numbers of bright, well-educated young evangelicals to do likewise. *Awakening the Evangelical Mind* offers a timely and important corrective to some of the popular misconceptions about modern evangelicalism, and it issues a fresh challenge to contemporary evangelical Christians to take up that important task yet again.

—Garth M. Rosell, Professor of Church History,
Gordon-Conwell Theological Seminary

AWAKENING *the* EVANGELICAL MIND

AWAKENING *the* EVANGELICAL MIND

An Intellectual History of the Neo-Evangelical Movement

OWEN STRACHAN

ZONDERVAN®

ZONDERVAN

Awakening the Evangelical Mind
Copyright © 2015 by Owen Strachan

This title is also available as a Zondervan ebook. Visit www.zondervan.com/ebooks.

Requests for information should be addressed to:

Zondervan, 3900 *Sparks Dr. SE, Grand Rapids, Michigan 49546*

Library of Congress Cataloging-in-Publication Data
Strachan, Owen.
    Awakening the evangelical mind : an intellectual history of the neo-evangelical
movement / Owen Strachan.
      pages cm
    Includes bibliographical references and index.
    ISBN 978-0-310-52079-5 (hardcover, jacketed)
    1. Evangelicalism—United States. 2. Ockenga, Harold John, 1905-1985. 3. Henry, Carl
F. H. (Carl Ferdinand Howard), 1913-2003. 4. United States—History—20th century. I.
Title.
BR1642.U5S77 2015
277.3'082—dc23   2015013918

Cover design: *Michelle Lenger*
Cover illustration: *123RF.com*
Interior design: *Denise Froehlich*

Printed in the United States of America

15 16 17 18 19 20 21 22 23 24 /DCI/ 20 19 18 17 16 15 14 13 12 11 10 9 8 7 6 5 4 3 2 1

To Douglas Sweeney, Greg Wills, and Patrick Rael

CONTENTS

The empires of the future are the empires of the mind.
—WINSTON CHURCHILL AT HARVARD, 1943

FOREWORD

For the better part of the last century, conservative Protestants in America have been finding their way in an increasingly alien and hostile culture. The full force of modernity, apparent even in the early decades of the twentieth century, led to the development of a movement among conservative Protestants in America that would eventually be called the neo-evangelical movement.

Interestingly, those later identified by sociologists as among the "knowledge class" were largely unaware of this development until *Newsweek* magazine declared 1976 the year of the evangelical. That cover story was a response to the fact that many in American academia, positions of influence, and cultural activism were shocked when it became apparent that a self-identified evangelical Christian was about to be elected president of the United States. Quite quickly, investigations were launched into the nature of evangelicalism and the movement behind it. In the main, the evangelical movement was explained to the nation in terms of conservative social activism and evangelistic fervor. Missing from that portrait is the story Owen Strachan tells so well in this new book. Indeed, the story he tells is a narrative of intellectual awakening, an awakening that took place among conservative Protestants in the aftermath of the fundamentalist-modernist controversy in the early twentieth century. One of the great strengths of Strachan's presentation of this story is his focus on Harold John Ockenga and Carl F. H. Henry, titanic figures on the neo-evangelical stage.

Simply by noting that influence, Strachan points to a significant gap in the way American intellectual history is most often told. What is almost entirely missing from the major narratives of intellectual history is the intellectual awakening that took place among conservative Christians in America, who came together at a specific moment in cultural history with a specific set of goals in mind.

Strachan tells the story of Ockenga and Henry very well. He places the evangelical intellectual awakening within the context of America at midcentury, and he rightly points to the collapse of conservative Protestant efforts in the fundamentalist movement. Fundamentalism, in the main, was forced into an institutional retreat. By the midpoint of the twentieth century, that retreat included readouts that included Bible colleges, a few publishing enterprises, and a network of Bible conferences.

Harold John Ockenga and Carl F. H. Henry looked at the rubble of conservative Protestantism and hoped for something better. Not only that, they specifically targeted conservative Protestant intellectual withdrawal as a key factor in the demolished hopes of the early twentieth century. Rather than retreat from the intellectual life of the nation, Ockenga and Henry intended to *engage* it. Intellectual engagement became the driving passion of this new evangelical movement. The larger and surpassing goals of the evangelical movement were, and remain, evangelistic. This is a movement that is established, before anything else, in the gospel of Jesus Christ. And yet Ockenga and Henry, along with those who would join them in the neo-evangelical movement, did not believe that conservative Christianity was faltering for lack of evangelistic fervor. Rather, they saw the central failing of the movement as an absence of intellectual vigor.

For this reason, the biographies of Ockenga and Henry are, in miniature, stories of intellectual aspiration and determination. Ockenga would eventually be called as the pastor of Boston's famed Park Street Church, but only after completing a PhD at the University of Pittsburgh. Henry, after earning a Doctorate of Theology from Northern Baptist Theological Seminary, would go on to earn a PhD at Boston University.

The narrative of twentieth-century evangelicalism cannot be recounted without careful attention to Harold John Ockenga and Carl F. H. Henry. In Strachan's account, both appear as the vivid historical characters they actually were. Ockenga appears as one of the last of the Boston Brahmins; Carl Henry appears as one of the last great empire builders. Strachan writes candidly about their aspirations and offers a critical evaluation of their successes and failures. He traces the points of intersection that brought Ockenga and Henry together, including, most important, the establishment of Fuller Theological Seminary. Ockenga appears as evangelicalism's "indispensable man," "without whom no major enterprise could be projected." Henry, on the other hand, appears as the journalist turned theologian turned writing dynamo who put evangelical convictions and hopes to voice.

Strachan traces Henry's failed hopes for a great evangelical university to be located in the Northeast, and he goes back to acknowledge the influence of Ockenga's conference for evangelical scholars held in Plymouth, Massachusetts, long before anyone had dared hope of evangelical intellectual engagement that would catch secular attention.

Ockenga and Henry advocated for intellectual engagement that would not lead to a theological diminishment. To the end, both remained resolutely committed to evangelical truth, and this was the animating determination behind their mode of intellectual engagement.

It is high time that the story of the evangelical intellectual awakening be told, and this important book communicates an important part of that story very well. We are in debt to Owen Strachan for his careful consideration of both Ockenga and Henry, and for his care in placing these men and the movement they so powerfully shaped within the context of twentieth-century American intellectual life.

And yet there is far more to be told. My great hope is that this work will serve as a catalyst for a renaissance of evangelical studies, a renaissance that will contribute toward the shaping of an intellectual awakening among evangelicals in the present and future, even as we learn from the past.

I am very thankful that I came to know Carl F. H. Henry as both mentor and friend. I greatly regret that I never had the opportunity to know Harold John Ockenga. And yet I do believe this book will allow any interested reader to come to know both Ockenga and Henry— and the movement they led—in a whole new light. May evangelicals who read this book be inspired to contribute to an evangelical awakening the likes of which the world has not yet seen.

—R. Albert Mohler Jr.

ACKNOWLEDGMENTS

Ryan Pazdur of Zondervan helped greatly in the formation of this monograph. He shared my vision for a scholarly work that would tell, in an accessible but thoroughgoing way, the neo-evangelical intellectual story. Stan Gundry gave valuable perspective on the era and carefully read through the manuscript, offering numerous helpful insights.

My colleagues at Southern Seminary and Boyce College lent strength during my writing. The generous leadership of R. Albert Mohler Jr., Randy Stinson, and Dan DeWitt make it possible for faculty members to devote serious amounts of time to worthy projects. I am especially thankful to Dr. Mohler for his foreword. He has been a profound intellectual influence on me.

At Bowdoin College, Sarah McMahon, Daniel Levine, Paul Nyhus, and Susan Tanenbaum trained me in academic history. At the Southern Baptist Theological Seminary (SBTS), Tom Nettles, Shawn Wright, and Michael Haykin gave me the model of scholar-churchman I wanted. So too at Trinity Evangelical Divinity School, where John Woodbridge, Scott Manetsch, and Ken Minkema (visiting professor) aided my formation as a historian. Dr. Woodbridge proffered many profitable chestnuts about neo-evangelicalism. George Marsden, external reader on my dissertation committee, gave me both his time and his own body of work as a model. Garth Rosell showed me considerable generosity in my research in the Ockenga archives at Gordon-Conwell Theological Seminary. What gold there is in dusty boxes.

Douglas Sweeney, my doctoral advisor at TEDS, trained me

through his judicious writing, his numerous courses, and his friend-ship. Gregory Wills of SBTS taught me a masterful survey of church history while occasionally interrupting himself to dig into lesser-known matters of the past. Patrick Rael of Bowdoin introduced me to the concept of history as a contest of ideas, a combustible and thrilling clash of visions. To these three scholars I dedicate this book.

I am grateful to my wife, Bethany, who supported and encour-aged me over years of work on this manuscript. My family, both the Strachan and Ware sides, were a great help to me. My parents, Andrew and Donna Strachan, nurtured my intellectual curiosities as a child, for which I will always be thankful.

Finally, to the God who is as much the author of history as he is the author of his authoritative Word, I may only offer gratitude for awakening my own evangelical mind.

INTRODUCTION

In the early twenty-first century, Alvin Plantinga is a world-famous philosopher. Not long ago, toward the end of the twentieth century, he emerged as one of the most prominent intellectual spokespersons for theism. A tall, wizened, bespectacled man, Plantinga publicly tangled with "New Atheists" like Richard Dawkins, was profiled by the *New York Times*, and occupied an endowed chair at the University of Notre Dame. On the campus featuring "Touchdown Jesus," few would have mistaken Plantinga for a football player. But he had established himself as a cagey competitor in the realm of worldview conflict. Plantinga often deployed his theories of "possible worlds" and "properly basic beliefs" with a slightly mischievous look on his face. He seemed to relish the opportunity to defend Christianity before its philosophical detractors.

Plantinga was not always an intellectual celebrity with a twinkle in his eye. He underwent extensive preparation for his excursions with Sam Harris and Daniel Dennett. In 1957, his colleagues at Wayne

State University in Detroit, Michigan, doubted his intelligence. The man who hired Plantinga gave voice to these doubts, or at least to his skepticism over whether any intelligent person could be a Christian. Plantinga was surprised by this response. He had been raised in the richly theological Dutch Reformed tradition and thought himself well-prepared for the environment he entered in 1957. His doctoral work at Yale University rendered him, at the very least, an intelligent person and able teacher. Or so he thought.

The Wayne State department chair, George Nakhnikian, disagreed with his young faculty member's self-conception. Plantinga later remembered Nakhnikian's disdain for Christianity: "Nakhnikian was our chairman; he thought well of my powers as a budding young philosopher but also thought that no intelligent person could possibly be a Christian." The matter came up on occasion, with a standard repartee ensuing, according to Plantinga: "He would announce this sentiment in his usual stentorian tones, whereupon Robert Sleigh would say, 'But what about Al, George? Don't you think he's an intelligent person?' George would have to admit, reluctantly, that he thought I probably was, but he still thought there had to be a screw loose in there somewhere."[1]

Plantinga recalled the remark in humorous terms as he reflected on his career in philosophy later in life. He obviously enjoyed the intellectual gamesmanship back in his proving-ground days, just as he relished it late in his career. Yet Plantinga noted that Nakhnikian had a point. Very few bona fide evangelical philosophers plied their trade in 1957: "When I left graduate school in 1957, there were few Christian philosophers in the United States, and even fewer Christian philosophers willing to identify themselves as such. Had there been such a thing as the Society of Christian Philosophers, it would have had few members." Most philosophers in the academy shared Nakhnikian's mindset, Plantinga suggested, for "an intelligent and serious philosopher couldn't possibly be a Christian. It looked as if Christianity would have an increasingly smaller part to play in the academy generally and in philosophy specifically; perhaps it would dwindle away altogether."[2]

By 2011, the Notre Dame professor's tune had changed. Speaking with the *New York Times*, Plantinga noted a remarkable shift over the years in his profession. "There are vastly more Christian philosophers and vastly more visible or assertive Christian philosophy now than when I left graduate school," he told the reporter. Despite his central location in this renaissance, he concluded, "I have no idea how it happened."[3]

Plantinga's story has its own contours, its own twists and turns. But the phenomenon recognized by the philosopher relates to a broader historical development in twentieth-century American life. Evangelicals, once associated with an uncritical, anti-intellectual state of mind, have in the last several decades reentered the academy. Where their forebears once made separation from secularism a mark of piety, many modern evangelicals take pride in their connection to elite institutions. This has proved surprising to members of the academy and the intelligentsia, many of whom have only recently discovered the species of *Evangelicalus Academius*.

This rare find has fascinated the highbrow West. In 2000, the *Atlantic Monthly* commissioned a long-form essay stretching more than ten thousand words from Alan Wolfe of Boston College. The essay, titled "Opening of the Evangelical Mind," charted the new evangelical zeitgeist. According to him, Christian scholars were "writing the books, publishing the journals, teaching the students, and sustaining the networks necessary to establish a presence in American academic life."[4] In Wolfe's estimation, figures like Mark Noll, Plantinga, and Cornelius Wolterstorff showed that "the rest of America cannot continue to write off conservative Christians as hopelessly out of touch with modern American values."

It was apparent to Wolfe, himself a religious scholar, that evangelicals—at least some of them—had genuinely bought into the life of the mind. For an *Atlantic* readership that snickered when President

22

George W. Bush named Jesus Christ his favorite philosopher and that could call to mind the intellectually laughable testimony of William Jennings Bryan in the Scopes Monkey Trial, this was strange fire.

The species yet lives. In his incisive 2007 study of the late-modern evangelical project of cultural engagement, *Faith in the Halls of Power*, sociologist D. Michael Lindsay suggested that "[t]he visibility of evangelical intellectualism has grown remarkably in a relatively short time."[5] Lindsay pointed to the success of programs like the Evangelical Scholars Project, an initiative of the Pew Charitable Trust, which supported the high-level publishing efforts of evangelical scholars like Noll, James Davison Hunter, Joel Carpenter, Robert Wuthnow, and many others. A rising academic star in his own right (and now president of Gordon College), Lindsay went so far as to assert that "evangelicals are well on their way" to "the intellectual mainstream."[6] We might amend the prevailing question in the academic halls of power. It may no longer be, "Where have all these Christians come from?" but, "Why are all these Christians still here?"

The foregoing begs a more elemental question, though: Is there any historical background to this modern phenomenon? Several of the projects mentioned thus far reference a pack of midcentury Protestants who called themselves the "new evangelicals." Led by pastor Harold Ockenga, theologian Carl Ferdinand Howard Henry, and evangelist Billy Graham, the neo-evangelicals championed a freshly intellectual and culturally engaged brand of evangelicalism that broke with the separationist, preeminently defensive program of fundamentalism.

These three figures, and many of their peers, whom we will meet in pages to come, were dyed-in-the-wool theological conservatives who lived and moved and had their being among the sprawling fundamentalist and evangelical worlds of the early and mid-twentieth century. In chapters 1 and 2, we meet Harold John Ockenga, the premier institution-builder of the period. The well-heeled Boston pastor promoted a doctrinally orthodox yet culturally aware Christianity through such institutions as the National Association of Evangelicals (NAE, founded in 1942), the aforementioned Fuller Seminary (ca. 1947), and *Christianity Today* (ca. 1956, with Henry as editor-in-chief).[7] Ockenga was the first president of the NAE, Fuller, and Gordon-Conwell Theological Seminary, and he was the founding chairman of the board of *Christianity Today*.

Ockenga's name has slipped the evangelical memory. In his time, however, he was a movement leader of nearly unparalleled influence. If, as James Davison Hunter has suggested, institutions powered by well-connected individuals drive social and cultural change, then in our day Ockenga must be reevaluated and restored to the position of prominence he enjoyed in his own.[8] No other figure save for Graham played a larger role in envisioning the cornerstone institutions of neo-evangelicalism; no figure, *including* Graham, did more than Ockenga to run, establish, and invigorate the premier institutions of the movement.

But we cannot stop there. We must also connect Ockenga to a larger but underappreciated group of scholars introduced in chapters 3 and 4 as the Cambridge evangelicals, a group of scholars who made an intellectual pilgrimage to Cambridge in the 1940s. This was a coterie of tremendous promise; among its band of future evangelical leaders were Henry, Edward John Carnell, Kenneth Kantzer, and George Eldon Ladd. These and nearly a dozen other peers of similar make enrolled at the university to gain elite training and credentials.[9] In successive decades and from a range of institutions, the scholars extended the project through academic ventures and literary initiatives that championed a fresh approach to non-Christian culture and thought.

Scholarly study and analysis of Ockenga and the Cambridge evangelicals yields new insights for the questions posed earlier. While there are doubtless other factors that help account for the modern-day evangelical academic awakening, chapters 5 and 6 make plain that the story of the opening of the evangelical mind cannot be told without significant reference to Ockenga, Henry, Graham, Carnell, and the Cambridge evangelicals. The most famous of this group are cited often in historiographical discussions, though at present little original archival material has gone public.

This text features intellectual history by way of social history. It charts the academic development of an entire movement by first investigating Ockenga's capacious scholarly vision. It details how his prestigious pastorate at Boston's Park Street Church functioned as his platform for broader leadership. It lends perspective on the young scholars' experience in Boston. It spells out how the diverse connections between Ockenga and scholars like Henry played a major role in the intellectual recalibration of evangelicalism. It tells the underappreciated story of several projects launched with leaders like Billy Graham that helped initiate the broader undertaking in question. These include the Plymouth Scholars' Conferences (chapter 4), publishing projects (chapter 5), *Christianity Today* (chapter 6), the Evangelical Theological Society (chapter 6), and Crusade University (chapter 6).

In *Awakening the Evangelical Mind*, we eavesdrop on the founding fathers of scholarly neo-evangelicalism as they share their frustration with one another over fundamentalism's perceived academic shortcomings. We see their intellectual insecurity, their sometimes preening ambition, their considerable interest in proving themselves before a non-Christian audience that likely took less stock of the group than they might have wanted to admit.[10] This is a quixotic, lively, and conflicted story. It is full of contradictions and paradoxes.

What successes the movement did achieve came at a cost felt in at least three ways. First, the drive to create a new scholarly literature and win a newly intellectual reputation brought tremendous strain to several of the Cambridge evangelicals. Though later generations of Christian academics cite figures like Carnell and George Eldon Ladd as models for their own vocations, it is clear that these and other scholars suffered under the burden of their ambitions. Further, while neo-evangelicalism is referenced positively today as a transdenominational project by evangelical leaders like Tim Keller and Gregory Thornbury—both call it "classic evangelicalism"—its founders struggled to find common ground as the years wore on.[11]

Last, when Mark Noll sketched a narrative of evangelicalism at the end of the twentieth century, he noted some positive scholarly efforts of Ockenga, Henry, and their peers, but famously concluded that there still was not "much of an evangelical mind."[12] There was and is truth to this conclusion, not least because with a movement so diverse and divided, it can be challenging to identify a distinctly Christian intellect.

Noll's famous judgment should not obscure the real accomplishments of the Cambridge scholars in particular and the neo-evangelicals in wider lens. The mid-century attempt to reengage the life of the mind represents the most significant intellectual development among American Christians since the institutional heyday of the eighteenth and nineteenth centuries, when countless American colleges and universities were founded. In sum, Ockenga, Graham, Henry, and their peers left a major mark on American Christianity. In the estimation of Keller, Thornbury, and others, they offer a model, however flawed, of how Christians—more broadly, religious persons—may honestly and passionately engage their culture. This model is worth studying on its own terms, for it was influential in its day.

This material is thus not only historically important but contemporarily relevant. Modern evangelicals find themselves in a cultural location that is remarkably similar to that occupied by the prewar church some seventy-five years ago. The spirit of George Nakhnikian, it seems, has not disappeared in our day. If anything, academic distrust of Christians has grown only more pervasive in America. For their part, evangelicals are increasingly perceived as behind the times. Despite cultural marginalization, the broader movement continues to survive and, in its more confessional corners, thrive. Part of the reason for this tenacity is the evangelical commitment to spiritually vital institutions, including institutions that seek to hand down the "faith that was once for all delivered to the saints" (Jude 3). Evangelicals, like their Jewish, Catholic, and Mormon counterparts, are used to the rough-and-tumble exchange of the American experiment.

Yet though they are a fibrous people, and though they have a zeal for academic entrepreneurship, evangelicals have not always excelled at being a thinking people. This reality makes the story of the Cambridge scholars all the stranger and all the more valuable. In the material that follows, we tell the unexpected but gripping story of how, in the most intellectually challenging season conservative American Protestants had ever known, a season when its academic prospects seemed all but lost, the evangelical mind awakened.

CHAPTER 1

BOSTON BRAHMIN IN TRAINING

The Preparation of Harold Ockenga

Many years before he became one of the last of the Boston Brahmins, a card-carrying member of the Massachusetts elite, Harold Ockenga sat down to pen his girlfriend a letter. The year was 1929. The days when an American president would write him a congratulatory note on the occasion of his retirement were far off; the late nights when he founded institutions from thin air were a distant prospect. Later on, Ockenga would become the Protestant pastor *par excellence* of his generation, thundering in his gravelly bass from Boston's most prestigious pulpit to an audience sprinkled with Harvard professors, MIT researchers, and globe-trotting businesspeople. In October 1929, Ockenga's star had yet to rise to these heights. He had no major work to lead, no landmark speech to give; he had a girlfriend to woo.

This is not to say, however, that he wrote in a quiet season. Ockenga found himself caught in one of the greatest cultural battles of his day. He was a young student at Princeton Theological Seminary, then roiled by conflict between Presbyterian conservatives and moderates. He said as much to Virginia Ray, his long-distance girlfriend: "Well, when I came back I found all these internationally known professors and all my friends going to the new seminary. It was a case of taking a stand for Christ against the modernist encroaches upon Princeton." This "new seminary" was Westminster Theological Seminary, just founded by theologian J. Gresham Machen.[1] It sounded like dark days ahead for his current school: "Princeton has changed and can never be the same, so they set forth to organize a new seminary which would be true to God's Word."[2]

Ockenga's reflection shows a young man in the flush of theological discovery. Princeton had cast a spell upon the budding preacher, as other letters and diary entries show. But Gothic buildings and endless library stacks were not the point of Ockenga's education, as he said to Virginia: "To me my ambition is primarily to be a man of God. To do this I must know how to preach, pray and live. Everything else must bow to that or go."[3] Ockenga had set his face to the plow. He was going to be a pastor, and a conservative one at that. It was the Roaring Twenties, but the nightclub scene in Manhattan—a short train ride from Princeton—held no interest for the pious seminarian. He wanted to preach and minister and turn the world upside down for Christ.

At this early stage in his career, Ockenga witnessed a watershed event in twentieth-century religious history: the final break of the so-called Presbyterian fundamentalists from the self-professed Presbyterian modernists. This was world creation, the birth of a new star, a confessional planet emerging *ex nihilo* from a bewildering and exhilarating struggle. The lesson of the epochal moment was not lost on the budding leader: for theologically conservative evangelicals, fidelity to Scripture required "taking a stand." This stated conviction, even at such a young point in Ockenga's life, is noteworthy. Though historians must be careful not to read historical documents like tea leaves, we note the location from which Ockenga sent his love letter to

Ray: South Pasadena, California. In this very city eighteen years later, Ockenga and several neo-evangelical colleagues would launch *sui generis* Fuller Theological Seminary to repel "modernist encroaches" and fashion a new apologetic for a modern day. Ockenga's letter to a Midwestern flame bore signs of a movement to come, one that would change the face of American Christianity.

Long before he wrote from Pasadena, Harold John Ockenga called Chicago home. He was born on June 6, 1905, to a middle-class family, the only son of Herman and Angie (Tetzlaff) Ockenga. Ockenga was raised in the Methodist church by his mother. From an early age, Ockenga exhibited a spark that set him apart from other children. The pastor's first biographer, ministry associate Harold Lindsell, comments on an early moneymaking venture of his: "Harold inherited energy and ambition from his parents, and turned toward the production of income when most other boys turned away from it. When nine years old, he got a Saturday job delivering orders for a grocery store, working from 8:00 in the morning to 9:00 or 10:00 at night."[4] Ockenga applied this same intensity to academic and religious ends throughout his early life. He finished high school in three and a half years even as he worked numerous jobs after his classes were over.

Ockenga was spiritually serious from a young age. This was true even before he experienced his "conversion" in high school. One hears echoes of the spiritual backstory of another luminary New England preacher, Jonathan Edwards, in Ockenga's preconversion narrative. Edwards built a prayer booth in the woods, essentially finding recreation in religion. Ockenga revved at a similar speed, cycling between no less than six different church services each Sunday.[5] His curiosity in religious matters was voracious, despite the fact that key members of his family, including his father, showed little interest in such pursuits.

It was during high school, just after World War I ended, that Ockenga professed faith in Jesus Christ. He later reflected on the event in a *Who's Who* application, reminiscing that his "conversion took place in an older boys' conference in Galesburg, Illinois, which I attended as a delegate from the Austin Methodist-Episcopal Church." His conversion "constituted a radical change in my life and the immediate consecration of myself to the Christian ministry. For over forty years I have never once doubted the reality of that conversion." Ockenga read the experience in terms consistent with views developed over the years in circles influenced by Keswick theology. (This theological school emphasized the importance of a full-hearted commitment to God alongside a profession of faith, itself achieved in a crisis moment.) The young man "experienced the critical coming of the Holy Spirit in His fullness whereby the New Testament level of spiritual life became a reality." He underlined this second spiritual development, giving it nearly as much weight as his coming to faith: "This was a critical experience following my conversion."[6]

After high school, Ockenga matriculated at Taylor University in Indiana. Taylor was a growing Christian college in the midst of a building phase. At the school, Ockenga developed a love for literature that led him to major in English. He enjoyed the curriculum, which focused on leading literary lights of the Western tradition. John Marion Adams has noted that, compared with other majors he considered entering, "His courses in English introduced him to a broader liberal arts curriculum. As an English major, Ockenga wrote papers on William Shakespeare, Robert Browning, Dante Alighieri, Christopher Marlowe, Johann Wolfgang Goethe, Nathaniel Hawthorne, and Victor Hugo."[7] This engagement with the *belles letres* marked the formal beginning of Ockenga's lifelong interest in the life of the mind. In sermons in later years, he frequently referenced these and other writers of consequence.

Ockenga's inquisitive mind was matched by an active conscience. At times, his strict code of personal ethics brought him into conflict with fellow classmates and his own aesthetic impulse. We gain a sense for how the romantic and the religious clashed in the young Ockenga in an early *credo* statement on the moral problems posed by collegiate drama.[8] In a missive that bears perhaps a trace of theatricality, Ockenga declared to his journal: "I have taken a stand this week against the dramatic work in Taylor University. Our class decided to pick out a play and asked me to play in one of the roles. I declined twice." No doubt Ockenga's classmates glimpsed a flair for the stage in him. But it was not to be; his "Here I stand" attitude extended beyond his refusal to act in the play: "Then this week they urged me to help in the decoration of stage, etc. I refused to do so. Now I must face the attitude I must take toward all drama and movies."[9] In successive decades, Ockenga never lost his penchant for dramatic remarks in pregnant moments.

Ockenga's intense faith did not detract from his studies. During his time at Taylor, he attained a 94 average and qualified for a Rhodes Scholarship nomination that proved unsuccessful.[10] He found joy not in the classroom, though, but in training for vocational ministry. The future homiletician joined a "preaching team" while in college and decided to pursue the ministry as a vocation after graduation.[11] Soon preaching occupied a great deal of Ockenga's free time. He thrilled to the preaching style of a renowned fundamentalist Baptist pastor named I. M. Haldeman. Haldeman was pastor of the First Baptist Church of New York City (1884–1933) and led the church to unparalleled prestige. His forceful fundamentalist style drew a reporter from the *New York Times* who described Haldeman for his readership: "Mr Haldeman, who is apparently about 35 years old, is a tall, spare man, with light hair and complexion and rather angular features. With exceeding fluency and vehemence of speech, he combines remarkable energy of gesticulation, vivid description, and decidedly dramatic action." Haldeman's physical engagement was most notable of all: "Many of his gestures are weird and some of them positively startling."[12]

The weirdness worked, apparently. Under Haldeman's leadership, the church grew steadily. Ockenga looked to the New York pastor as a mentor-from-afar and was drawn to his model of iconoclastic homiletics in an urban center. His classmates labeled Ockenga a "Haldemantal," so great was his allegiance.[13] While his collegiate peers at secular institutions sampled the hedonic pleasures of campus life, Ockenga barnstormed across the Midwest with a few friends to speak at youth conferences and preach in churches. Ockenga was determined to make himself a first-rate homiletician and Christian leader. He was young, committed, and ambitious, willing to push his body to its limits for the purposes of ministry.

As Ockenga and his peers drove for hours to preach all over the Midwest, he carried on a long-distance correspondence with the aforementioned Virginia Ray.[14] On December 17, 1926, Harold wrote Virginia from Almond, New York: "First in the east and then in the west, we go wherever the people are blessed. It's a good life of new things every day.. . . We hope to have a great revival. Thank God for the opportunity of preaching his loving, wonderful, thrilling gospel."[15] Ockenga's jaunty prose speaks to the evangelistic fervor of the youth culture of his milieu. He had tapped into the ministry circuit and had found his passion. For the rest of his life, Ockenga would preach the "thrilling gospel" of Christ crucified and risen for humanity's deliverance even as he constantly sought out "new things" through a peripatetic life of travel, speaking, and organizing.[16]

Ockenga preached not only in churches across the Midwest but also in his letters to his girlfriend. He was a model of earnest spiritual intensity. At one point, Ockenga unpacked at considerable length Virginia's need for a new "experience of sanctification." In preparation for the coming of a prominent Holiness itinerant, Harold wrote that "in his message Sunday he will speak of the experience of sanctification. This is what I am praying and trusting that you will soon see the need of and receive." He concluded the matter portentously: "It has been what has meant most in my life and I do so want you to receive Him."[17] There was not a little relational pressure in this spiritual exhortation.

Ockenga never wavered in his belief in a "second blessing"

experience in the years that followed. While at Princeton, he argued to his journal that if the blessing "has not been received at conversion it *must be* received before the entrance to heaven" and that while "the crucifixion and death [of the sinful heart] takes place at conversion," the "filling of the Spirit comes when the consecration is made either then or otherwise."[18] Though raised as a Methodist, trained under the mantle of Presbyterian Old Princeton, and identified early on as a potential leader of a stately New England Congregationalist church, Ockenga always emphasized that the Spirit's coming enabled victorious, powerful Christian living.[19] The neophyte evangelist ended up being J. Gresham Machen's foremost protégé, but he never lost the independent streak that surfaced early in his life and played an animating role in his more famous exploits.

Ockenga showed an unusual self-awareness in his college years. He knew that he was too busy and commented in his journal: "The fundamental cause of many of them is that I have kept too many irons in the fire. I have tried too many things and hence have been mediocre in most all."[20] The charge of "mediocrity" may have been harsh, but Ockenga's self-assessment of his busy life was prescient. Ockenga always overflowed with energy and struggled to contain it. But he was not undisciplined. Even as he confessed—and cursed—his inability to relax, he charted a course for himself that was highly unusual for his day.

Though the collegian wanted to jump into full-time ministry in his early twenties, he confessed to his journal that "there will be a greater glory for Him in my remaining hard at work in schools for seven more years till I have several advanced degrees and meanwhile keeping very close in touch with the work by means of revivals, conferences, and preaching."[21] This plan of action was remarkable. In an age when a sizeable portion of theologically conservative Christians did indeed choose ministry over academic training, Ockenga expressed a desire to accrue "several advanced degrees," a path that would take years to accomplish. Ockenga did not want merely to be an informed pastor.

He wanted, in some vaguely defined sense, to be a leader of pastors, an intellectual authority in his community. Many of his friends were content with a two-year diploma from a Bible institute. Though Ockenga shared the zeal of his friends for on-the-ground ministry, he dreamed of greater things. It was his goal to be a movement leader.

This pathway to extraordinary accomplishment and influence would take thirteen years, not seven. The next stop in Ockenga's ambitious plan would take him to a far grander setting: storied—and embattled—Princeton Theological Seminary. Before he journeyed east, Ockenga graduated from Taylor in May 1927. Then, he went home to prepare for seminary and earn some spending money. He worked as a lifeguard, which was a typical Ockengan move: he gravitated toward a setting that might have proved tempting to him but, once there, charted a moral course for himself. Over the rest of his life, Ockenga would sport an enviable tan in the summer months, but it was not the beach and its visitors that held his attention. It was his Greek vocabulary cards, as he said to Virginia: "I have arranged it so that my lifeguards do all my work during the swim and I sit in a tower they just erected for me and study Greek. That way I get over a lesson a day. I am making good headway and shall be in good shape to take my entrance at P- in the fall." One language was not enough, however. Ockenga was taking lessons in German from a professor "to start me toward my Ph.D. work."[22] He had not yet begun his postgraduate work but was already hard at work on his doctoral requirements.

After a busy summer that included an evangelistic message aimed at his unbelieving father, Ockenga set out for Princeton. Arriving in the town of Princeton in the full flowering of fall, he could not help but gush: "Everything is gothic," he wrote to Ray. "It makes one feel as though he lived back in the fourteenth century. Even the lights are so arranged. I expected much but it has passed all my expectations. It is cultured to the enth degree. Nothing I have ever seen can compare with it. No wonder it is rated as it is."[23]

Princeton was a magisterial enigma for the pious Taylor graduate. The seminary blended religious devotion and worldly attainment in a style that Ockenga had never seen before. He was dazzled by the school's medieval feel, its massive stone structures, and above all its intellectual horsepower. The student accustomed to working-class Chicago and the quiet isolation of a small Midwestern school had stepped into the world of high culture and elite instruction. Everywhere were resources ripe for the homiletical plucking. "Never shall I run out of sermon material after seeing the sources here," Ockenga gushed upon first arriving in New Jersey. "I readily perceive that three years will only introduce me to the host of material available for the preachers use."[24]

There was a seductive pull to Princeton that Ockenga sensed from his earliest arrival. This pull was invigorating, for the life of the mind pulsed at the institution, inviting intelligent students like Ockenga to lose themselves in the contemplation of ideas. But Ockenga could not abandon himself to Princeton. He found its enlightened, morally-liberated climate problematic. He did not know what to make of his worldly classmates, for example. Even at the seminary, they were "as a rule princely but far from deep in spiritual truths." He did not note the pun in his aside, but he did offer his own catalogue of worldliness at the school:

1. Dancing 10%
2. Smoking 30% or more
3. Swearing 5% (occasionally)
4. Constant theater attenders 70%
5. Card players 50%—(anywhere from Roche to Strip Poker)
6. Studying on Sunday 60% at least
7. Everybody talks of big churches and salaries but never hear of soul salvation
8. Never once have I been approached about my soul's condition
9. No vital piety
10. Strife in faculty[25]

These were strong words from a man who evidently loved his surroundings. It was clear that Ockenga's Holiness background and intense spirituality contrasted with the mindset of many students and faculty members at the university and also the seminary. His peers, ostensibly training for ministry, seemed to Ockenga to favor success, but not spirituality, and salaries, but not "soul salvation."

Ockenga did not worry long over this situation. He could not—he was too busy. As in his college days, travel took up a surprising amount of his time. He journeyed throughout the east and went to California, all while a student. In the fall of 1927, for example, he took a trip that foreshadowed his future course. To Virginia, he reported on November 15, 1927, that "this week I went to Boston and took in the sights. I saw Harvard, Boston Theo. Sem., Philips Brook's old church, the Commons, Wellesley, The Wayside Inn (where a party of us dined).. . .It was certainly interesting."[26] Later on, the Commons would become more than a curiosity; they would be the very setting for his ministry.

His peregrinations notwithstanding, Ockenga did not neglect his studies. He worked hard, in particular, at mastering the homily. A section of class notes from his preaching notebook provides an early snapshot of the homiletician-in-training. In a class with J. R. Smith held in the fall term of 1928–29 in Alexander Hall, Ockenga gave one of his first sermons before his colleagues and professor. His text was Matthew 19:16, in which a Pharisee approached Jesus as he approached the city of Jerusalem "and said unto him, 'Good Master, what good thing shall I do, that I may have eternal life?'" Ockenga's little black notebook records his sermon outline, a veritable model of alliterative terseness:

> INTRODUCTION: THE ONE WHO CAME
> 1. Claim to Deity
> 2. Condemnation of men
> 3. Came himself

Theme: The Man who Missed God Outline

1. The Law Kept
   a. Statement of it
   b. The interpretation of it
   c. The keeping of it
2. The lack confessed
   a. He wouldn't say he was a sinner
   b. He didn't know he was saved
   c. He confessed his need
3. The lesson in completeness
   a. Sell out
   b. Give to poor
   c. Follow me[27]

The sermon drew memorable critique. One of Ockenga's classmates suggested he temper his "speed mania" and "Methodist mournful sound."[28] His instructor noted that the sermon was "very good," that "[f]ollowing Christ is the essence of the gospel," and that it would be "more effective if slower," which might have functioned effectively as broader life advice.[29]

Ockenga showed great promise in his biblical studies classes. He entered a Greek contest in 1928–29 and won first place for his exegesis of Romans 11:1–2. The prize came with a one-hundred-dollar award, a hefty sum.[30] As his classes piled up, the young scholar voiced to his journal a growing academic confidence grounded in a desire to preach the Bible. "With English, German and French I can preach in almost any country today. Then with a reading knowledge of Latin, Greek, and Hebrew I am prepared investigate [*sic*] the classics and the historic setting of Christianity." He was pleased with his efforts to date: "With this background and the preparation of the coming five years I believe that I may be ready for a life of service and usefulness to my Lord."[31]

Ockenga's heady plans notwithstanding, Princeton and the Presbyterian denomination it served found itself in a massive conflict.

The conflict revolved around the question of confessional identity. Was Presbyterianism and its flagship seminary *modernist* by nature, a religious entity in step with the prevailing intellectual trends of the day? Or was Presbyterianism and Princeton skewing *fundamentalist*, as the modernists alleged, consigning itself to irrelevance by adhering to a rigorously literal interpretation of the Bible that created conflict with modern thought? This question raged throughout the 1920s and into the 1930s at the school and in the Presbyterian Church USA.[32]

Ockenga's journal and letters of the period offer limited comment on this controversy, which had simmered for some time among northern Presbyterians and the broader Christian world. For our purposes, the debate deserves some elaboration, for it led to the restructuring of the evangelical world and launched young pastors like Ockenga out of established networks and into new associations of their own formation.

In the late nineteenth century, the heresy trials of figures like Crawford Howell Toy of the Southern Baptist Theological Seminary in 1879 and Charles Augustus Briggs of Union Theological Seminary in 1892 led to the excommunication of these influential professors from their denominations.[33] Awareness of the methods and conclusions of liberal Christianity spread as a result of these trials and led many theologically conservative evangelicals to distrust historical criticism and liberal Christian theology. The scions of Old Princeton, B. B. Warfield and Charles Hodge, promoted awareness of these trends and offered stern critique of them in journals like the *Presbyterian Review* and the *Princeton Review*, for decades the mouthpiece of confessional conservatism.[34]

The increasing popularity of the "social gospel" in the early twentieth century, as formulated by figures like Walter Rauschenbusch and Shailer Matthews of the University of Chicago, only raised the alarm for Christians who professed fidelity to the orthodox creeds and confessions of historic Christianity. In 1910, the Presbyterian Church of the USA (PCUSA) offered the "doctrinal deliverance" or "five-point deliverance" as a statement of essential orthodoxy to which all ministers had to assent even as they confessed their fidelity to the Westminster Confession of Faith.[35]

Between 1910–1913, a group of pastors and theologians launched a further response to the modernist trends by authoring a series of pamphlets titled *The Fundamentals: A Testimony to the Truth*, which articulated the traditional positions on doctrines like the inerrancy of Scripture, the virgin birth, the substitutionary atonement of Christ, and the veracity of biblical miracles. As George Marsden has noted, these booklets, bankrolled by Lyman and Milton Stewart and edited by A. C. Dixon of Moody Church and R. A. Torrey of Moody Bible Institute, "became a symbolic point of reference for identifying a 'fundamentalist' movement."[36] *The Fundamentals* spelled out the essential doctrines of doctrinally conservative Christianity and helped lay down the theological gauntlet.[37]

Further developments followed as the two sides hardened their stances. Princeton's stance on confessional Christianity shifted in the 1910s as J. Gresham Machen, the inheritor of Old Princeton's mantle, found his views challenged by his colleagues on the faculty. D. G. Hart has commented that for Machen in this period, the shift in theological orientation at Princeton marked nothing less than the passing of an epoch.[38] Machen would later become Ockenga's foremost mentor.

The conservatives took on a new label when in 1920 Curtis Lee Laws, a Baptist minister and editor of the *Watchman-Examiner*, used the neologism "fundamentalist," suggesting that such people "still cling to the great fundamentals" and do "battle royal" to defend them.[39] Douglas Sweeney has observed that this term, cast negatively in our day, was considered by Laws and others "a badge of honor."[40] This badge was called into question in 1922 by Harry Emerson Fosdick of the First Presbyterian Church of New York City. Fosdick, a talented preacher whose star rose meteorically in the 1920s as the fundamentalist-modernist controversy heated up, delivered a defiant sermon titled "Shall the Fundamentalists Win?" in which he criticized the doctrines of the virgin birth, inerrancy, and the second coming of Christ.[41] Clarence Macartney of the First Presbyterian Church of Pittsburgh responded to Fosdick's sermon with one called "Shall Unbelief Win?" and called on his denomination to censure Fosdick, which did not happen.[42]

The debate over the future of the Presbyterian movement centered in theology, much as each side maneuvered for control of the churches and schools. For conservatives, Machen's 1923 monograph *Christianity and Liberalism* crystallized the ideas in question. Machen argued that the differences between the two sides were grounded not in theological arcanae but in core doctrine:

> Christianity is based, then, upon an account of something that happened, and the Christian worker is primarily a witness. But if so, it is rather important that the Christian worker should tell the truth. When a man takes his seat upon the witness stand, it makes little difference what the cut of his coat is, or whether his sentences are nicely turned. The important thing is that he tells the truth, the whole truth, and nothing but the truth. If we are to be truly Christians, then, it does make a vast difference what our teachings are, and it is by no means aside from the point to set forth the teachings of Christianity in contrast with the teachings of the chief modern rival of Christianity.[43]

He concluded the point with an explosive distinction: "The chief modern rival of Christianity is 'liberalism,'" not secularist thought, for "Christianity is founded upon the Bible," while liberalism "is founded upon the shifting emotions of sinful men."[44] This led to one unalterable and deeply divisive conclusion: "[M]odern liberalism not only is a different religion from Christianity but belongs in a totally different class."[45]

Machen's polemic clarified the conservative stance and suggested to many Presbyterians that compromise would prove impossible, a conjecture made tangible by the repudiation of the five-point deliverance by nearly two hundred pastors in the Auburn Avenue Declaration of 1924.[46] From 1926–29, Princeton and its fate represented the center of debate among the PCUSA. As a microcosm of the larger controversy, the Princeton Seminary administration and faculty found themselves at odds. While each side embraced the *evangelical* label, D. G. Hart has suggested that they diverged in their interpretation of doctrine as Machen had suggested. "On the one side were strict Calvinists," Hart concludes, "a group that included Machen and the majority of professors (seven of eleven) and the majority of the board of directors (nineteen of twenty-eight), the body responsible for faculty and curriculum."[47] The other side looked to Charles Erdman, professor of theology and moderator of the Presbyterian General Assembly, and J. Ross Stevenson, president of the seminary, for leadership. These "moderate evangelicals" had won "a majority of the board of trustees (seventeen of twenty-two), the officers responsible for finances." The two sides traded barbs in official documents, with two separate commissions of 1925 and 1927 judging that Princeton remained within appropriate theological bounds set by the Westminster Confession and the school's doctrinal charter.

In 1927, the general assembly approved the 1927 report by a wide margin—503 to 323—and the table was set for the administrative reorganization and theological recalibration of Princeton, a next step ratified and actualized at the denominational meeting in 1929.[48] The school would shift its focus away from the traditional curriculum, which emphasized theology and the biblical languages, and move toward a more practically oriented body of courses and a less controversial position. These trends led Machen to take the dramatic step of founding a new seminary, Westminster Theological Seminary, a school named for the document that Machen and his fellow conservative Presbyterians believed had been compromised by the new stance of Princeton.[49]

Ockenga followed these developments, though he did not leave much commentary on the controversy in his journals and letters.

From the seclusion of summer break, he wrote to Virginia on July 27, 1929, of the results of the Presbyterian controversy: "Princeton Seminary has now split in two. And most of the old faculty are organizing a new seminary. It will be called 'Westminster.' Princeton will be in the hands of the modernists. It's a sad story. I do not know yet where I shall go next year. I did so want to graduate from Princeton, but if it is modern, I'm afraid my principles will turn me elsewhere. Most of my friends are going to the new seminary. What do you think I should do?"[50] As one can see, Ockenga held the common conservative or fundamentalist view of the controversy that emphasized the modern, or liberal, turn of the institution. Though his commentary on the Presbyterian schism is dispassionate, his experience of these events left a deep imprint on his mind.[51] Ockenga's coming of age at one of the epicenters of the fundamentalist-modernist controversy surely shaped him for the work he was to champion in the 1940s. The young scholar watched as the leaders of doctrinally conservative evangelicalism founded their own work in the wake of their defeat. His later program suggests a kind of recapitulation of this experience.

Ockenga enrolled at Westminster Theological Seminary in Glenside, Pennsylvania, in 1930–31. He excelled in his studies at Westminster and demonstrated a maturing intellect in his coursework, which included a book review of Boston University theology professor Borden Parker Bowne's *The Principles of Ethics*.[52] Bowne's "personalism" lacked an "objective" quality, the seminarian opined: "The traditional view of a Christian authority superimposing law upon the individual or the Kantian law of autonomy laid down by the legislative self, or the changing law of experience, are all more consistant [*sic*] than Bowne's ethical theory."[53] This interest in ethics and public Christianity persisted throughout Ockenga's life. It took substantial shape first in Ockenga's doctoral dissertation and later in his tenure as first president of the National Association of Evangelicals, founded to reposition the Christian perspective on pressing social issues.

In 1931, Ockenga graduated from Westminster. During his final semester, he secured a position as assistant pastor at the First Presbyterian Church of Pittsburgh, working under moderate conservative Clarence Macartney.[54] He began his work on September 1, 1930, though he took a senior pastorate at Point Breeze Presbyterian Church in Pittsburgh just months later, beginning his work there on May 8, 1931. Machen spoke at his ordination on January 28, 1931, at Pittsburgh's First Church, giving the pastoral charge. He wrote to Ockenga a week later that "I do feel profoundly thankful that the first graduating class of Westminster Seminary is represented by a man like you. I do feel great confidence that God has very rich blessings in store both for you and for those to whom you will be called to minister."[55] The two continued an affectionate correspondence over the years, with Machen steering "Ocky," as he called him, to pastures he thought green.

It is at this point that we glimpse another prong of Ockenga's development and theological program. The young pastor was trained in Methodist and Holiness circles that challenged passionate young Christians like Ockenga to evangelize and pursue a sanctified life. Under the tutelage of Machen and others, Ockenga entered more fully into the confessional intellectual tradition of historic Presbyterianism. Ockenga never lost his passion for evangelism and discipleship, but Machen's mentorship left Ockenga with a hunger for theological engagement. The Westminster graduate said as much to his mentor in his second year at Point Breeze: "Your friendship has proved a source of tremendous blessing in my life, especially in spiritual and intellectual things. I am but a weak echo of the things you have fought through. Even though they are my own because of passing through my personality, yet you are the instrument. And I shall always appreciate it."[56] Ockenga's respect for Machen bordered on veneration, and for good reason. Machen's guidance directed the course of the young pastor's life and positioned him for the upper reaches of evangelical leadership.

For his part, Machen counseled his pupil on numerous matters. Ockenga sought his advice in figuring out whether to take on the editorship of a student paper titled *Christian Faith and Life*. Machen suggested he saw special promise in Ockenga in urging against it: "I long to see you go forward to really great things in the Presbyterian Church, and I don't want to see you dissipate your energies or break down under too heavy a burden." Machen concluded with an ironic twist his admiring critic, H. L. Mencken, would have appreciated: "Frankly, I feel very hesitant about advising you. I have just put down certain desultory thoughts as they come. Possibly, to use a phrase dear to the Modernist soul, further light may 'break' upon me. If so, I will try to let the gleam reach even unto you. Meanwhile I am a good deal perplexed."[57]

At another point, Machen advised Ockenga not to write a book on "Buchmanism," the system advocated by Dr. Frank Buchman that centered in individual transformation engendered by total "surrender to God." A proponent of modern-day miracles rooted in the individual's direct access to God, Buchman made great waves in his day. He is essentially lost to history but was a fantastical figure in his own time. During the course of a several-decade career, Buchman helped found Alcoholics Anonymous, advised celebrities and nations on the doctrine of Moral Rearmament, landed on the cover of *Time*, and aided in the brokering of postwar peace between Germany and France in 1950.[58]

Buchman does not seem to have openly championed a heresy, but his work drew continual fire for its emphasis on "listening to God" and its vaguely defined theology. Ockenga took issue with it and sent a draft form of his critique to Machen, occasioning a lengthy and personal letter back that reveals the more personal, private side of the controversialist. Noting that "in certain places you verge upon the doctrine of 'second blessing', which does not seem to me to be Scriptural," Machen criticized Ockenga's analysis of Buchmanism: "In particular I know nothing whatever about the false intellectualism that you speak of at the beginning of your chapter on 'The Need which Gave Birth to Buchmanism'. On the contrary I remember in my youth a depreciation of doctrine the deadliness of which I did not at that time understand. Modernist (including Buchmanite) anti-intellectualism has cast its blight upon the church for a very long period now." He then discoursed on the subject of modernism:

> Here we are in a great fight between Christianity and Modernism. Some people are contending for the despised Christian position. They may have their faults, and of course do have their faults. But when we are in such a *tremendous battle* against a deadly enemy, would it not be better to give what comfort we can to the despised defenders of the Bible rather than use the miserable shibboleths of the enemy regarding them? I have the reputation of being a very censorious person, but my censoriousness is not exercised against people who are ready to say a good word for the Scriptures against the opponents of the Scriptures. I have considerable charity in my heart for them.

Machen penned his conclusion with a velvet glove: "I have such a very high ideal for you, and such an admiration for your Christian testimony, that I am anxious to see you do full justice to your splendid talents in everything that you publish."[59]

Ockenga quickly replied to his mentor: "Thank you for your clear criticism of the work on Buchmanism."[60] Chastened, he noted that he would "abandon for the present any idea of publishing this and simply put in pamphlet form the subjects that I have preached in order to answer the inquiries concerning the error and state my position upon it." The affair concluded with this resolve and nothing more was said of it between mentor and student.

Ockenga's line of correspondence with Machen unveils his intellectual development and his theological ties. Ockenga engaged disparate theological groups in his spiritual training, but his most intensive period of tutelage came from his interaction with Machen, the heir of Old Princeton. As he communicated with Ockenga over the years before his sudden death in 1937, Machen sought to pass on his theological perspective, and it is inarguable that Ockenga's Reformational convictions owe in large part to his time at Princeton and Westminster, where Machen was the foremost theologian. Under Machen, and at the seminaries he led, Ockenga embraced the Reformed tradition foreign to him in his earlier years. He would never leave it.

From his days at Taylor, Ockenga had hungered after a doctoral degree. Before beginning his ministry at Point Breeze, he had begun masters-level coursework at the University of Pittsburgh while ministering at the First Church. He filled Virginia in on his plans in early September 1930: "I'm starting in on the 20th at the University of Pittsburgh. I will accomplish two things there in the next year; get a M.A. in Arts and get my residence requirements off on a doctor's degree. Then I can take the rest of my work where I please." Here, as before, we see the native entrepreneurial instinct in young Ockenga. He did not wish to take a vow of poverty in ministry but was glad of having abundant resources on hand to accomplish his goals.[61]

Ockenga initially wanted to study at Princeton but was glad to do a PhD at a reputable school like Pitt. He plunged into his two-front life, focusing on completing his coursework in his allotted three years even as he sought to build the church. The young pastor noted in one of his breathless asides to Virginia that it represented "an advance in every way," whether considering his opportunity to preach weekly or the fact that he ministered in an ornate building with a massive steeple and a soaring spire.[62] As he preached and evangelized and served the midsized congregation of several hundred members, Ockenga discharged his spiritual ambitions. He continued his coursework at the university and worked under Professor Mont R. Gabbert, head of the department of philosophy at the school. The philosopher was a self-professed "religious man" and proved a critical though patient doctor-father to Ockenga.[63]

The church grew and the dissertation loomed. In the fall of 1932, Ockenga told Virginia some good news that showed that Point Breeze was growing in numbers: "Last Sunday we received 15 adults into membership. That makes 150 in 1 1/2 years."[64] This growth signified the achievement of one plank of Ockenga's vision. He evinced distaste at his Princeton classmates' hunger for salaries and large churches, but he himself craved influence and clearly took to a cosmopolitan life in his postcollege years. Ockenga was not alone in placing great importance on the size and pace of expansion of his congregation. This was the age when church growth became not only a spontaneous event but an established discipline in American seminaries, with figures like Gaines Dobbins of the Southern Baptist Theological Seminary applying business methods—and corporate expectations—to local assemblies in pursuit of larger membership.[65] In buying into this model, at least implicitly, Ockenga stood astride the old confessional world and the burgeoning religious marketplace of the future.

Ockenga had his dissertation to finish too. When he was not studying and strategizing for further growth, the young minister had to use late nights, weekends, and summer breaks to finish the thesis, which he completed to the satisfaction of his committee in 1939. Gabbert suggested the topic of the monograph to Ockenga in a course on social philosophy. It was, in the end, titled "Poverty as a Theoretical and Practical Problem of Government in the Writings of Jeremy Bentham and the Marxian Alternative." Ockenga had entered into a major contemporary debate over the nature of the government's role in addressing poverty.

He wrote in a guarded style throughout the text, devoting great amounts of space to the views of various camps on questions of poverty and government. In the end, he seemed to voice careful appreciation for the solution to poverty proposed by Bentham, the utilitarian who trained J. S. Mill and in his spare time designed prison systems: "The poorhouse as a method of treating the problem of poverty is practically abandoned. Simultaneously, poverty is no longer looked upon as a disgrace or a source of culpability."[66]

Ockenga did not finish the dissertation until well into his pulpit work at Park Street Church, but his reception of the degree signaled an impressive accomplishment. Unlike fellow students, Ockenga worked in full-time ministry for the duration of his doctorate, first at a prestigious church booming with new members, later at Boston's flagship evangelical congregation.[67] He never published it, and though his credentials gained him considerable credibility, he did not pursue the topic at length in future publishing. Even a glance at the 314-page document shows, however, that Ockenga had attained intellectual maturity. He had the ability to handle complex philosophical and social questions and address them at an expert level to the satisfaction of a secular audience. Ockenga had established that he was not merely interested in the life of the mind but was in fact a practitioner of it.[68] This accomplishment shaped his future work as much as any other.

Ockenga's achievement stood out in his day. This was a time when precious few of the clergy earned doctorates, especially secular doctorates. The educated clergy gravitated toward the urban pulpits. According to Brooks Holifield, among urban pastors in 1926, "14 percent graduated from college alone, 12 percent graduated from a seminary without having earned a college degree, and 28 percent had a high-school education or less."[69] Outside of the city, things shifted, as "in the largest denominations" between 24 and 27 percent "had a college and seminary education, and only 41 percent had graduated from college. Fully 50 percent had only a high-school education or less."[70] The picture sketched by Holifield underscores the significance of Ockenga's course of learning. His drive to attain a PhD, expressed even before he earned his bachelor's degree at Taylor, suggests something unique about the pastor in relation to the evangelical intellect. While Ockenga was surely an ambitious man, he seems to have had a genuine desire to equip his mind for the challenges of some form of intellectual leadership, whether of a church or a movement. His coursework, journal, and letters reveal a scholar-in-training who wished to continually buttress his learning.

Even before Ockenga graduated from the University of Pittsburgh, his hunger paid off. Ockenga's ability to draw members at Point Breeze and his matriculation at the university made him a strong candidate to pastor a leading church of American evangelicalism. As Ockenga preached and studied and wrote his missives to Virginia, Machen and others were conspiring behind the scenes to place Ockenga, the most impressive student Westminster had produced by the mid-1930s, in just the right pastoral position. Machen foresaw that Ockenga, though young, could likely take the lead of a prestigious urban congregation. Machen had trained him, read his work, and observed his strong leadership in Pittsburgh. What the Presbyterian statesman couldn't foresee was that Ockenga, in just a few short years, would become not simply a leading pulpiteer but the premier institution-builder of his era.

Before all of evangelicalism became his parish, though, Boston was.

CHAPTER 2

"A MIGHTY MAN OF GOD"

The Pastoral Work of Harold Ockenga

J. Gresham Machen was a man of the world. Raised in an upper-class Baltimore family, he was the most sophisticated of churchmen. Educated at Johns Hopkins University and Princeton Theological Seminary, Machen drifted through early adulthood. He flirted with German liberalism and inclined temperamentally toward skepticism. For years, Machen wrestled with doubts about Christianity. The faculty of Princeton Theological Seminary had their eye on him nonetheless. In 1906, after much wooing, he was hired to teach New Testament. As he embraced the duty of training pastors to teach the people of God, Machen warmed to his task. In time, Machen outpaced his Princeton faculty peers in arguing for the importance of traditional Presbyterian theology and polity.

But this was not to say Machen gave up his cigars and scotch. His insouciance lingered as well. It was said that when Machen grew bored with Greek recitations in class, he would stand up from his chair and softly bang his head on the chalkboard. At other times, he would open his mail or recite paradigms backward, to the confusion of his students. Machen was a character. But he was also a confessional strategist *par excellence.* His polemic promotion of conservative theology in the landmark *Christianity and Liberalism* rendered him a hero in the eyes of the conservative evangelical world. With this bold stance came great influence. If Machen took an interest in a young scholar or future pastor, he had the ability to launch his career into the ether.

This is precisely what happened with Harold John Ockenga, Machen's most gifted acolyte. In November 1934, Ockenga found himself in a place familiar to many an ambitious and talented young person: contemplating a move to another congregation, a mid-sized church also in the Northeast. Ockenga's work at Point Breeze Presbyterian Church had gone well over the previous three years by any respect. This was all the truer considering Presbyterianism had been locked in a struggle for the soul of the movement. Not many first-time ministers see hundreds of members added to the rolls in their first few years of pastoring, especially when the young pastor in question is completing a secular doctorate in philosophy.

From afar, Machen could see what was transpiring. It made perfect sense for the Pennsylvania church to seek Ockenga out. The elder statesman knew that many more such parishes would take a shine to the polished young man with a unique last name. But Machen recognized that Ockenga's gifts called for a wider influence, a more prestigious pulpit. As Machen traveled all over the country to stir up funds for Westminster, the Independent Board on Foreign Missions, and the fledgling Independent Presbyterian Church, he contemplated how to best deploy Ockenga for conservative ends.

In November 1934, Machen first told Ockenga of a prospect that would change the young man's life—and evangelicalism with it. Ockenga wrote to Machen to ask for advice on whether he should take a pastorate at the First Presbyterian Church of New Castle, Pennsylvania. Point Breeze had steadily grown, and he liked his post.

In his estimation, he had "a bigger sounding board in this smaller church here for the gospel than I'd have there." He was wrestling with the matter and suggested that "[i]t would be nice to be a Buchmanite at such a time as this."[1] Like many young pastors before and after him, he craved a kind of direct access to the mind and will of God for his decision.

Machen's reply to Ockenga was careful. "Ocky," wrote Machen, "I am inclined to think that your move to that church might be in itself a good strategic move," though he then hedged this already circum- spect encouragement: "There is an extremely important consideration which enters in." He elaborated on this consideration: "Advices that have come to me indirectly are to the effect that you are being con- sidered very prominently for the pastorate of the Park Street Church in Boston. That is not only a strategic post but it is a tremendous post." In a final line that must have gotten Ockenga's pastoral pulse going, he summed up the church's significance: "I think it is one of the two or three most important points in this country for real Christian testimony."[2]

Ockenga knew of Park Street. He had traveled to Boston while at Princeton and, like many of his peers, was familiar with Park Street and its famous pastor, A. Z. Conrad, himself a doctor of letters from a secular urban university. Conrad enjoyed great regional prestige in his day and was perhaps the informal mayor of Boston. He earned his PhD from the City College of New York, now New York University, in 1891. He had married into the family of John Adams, wedding Harriet Narcissa Adams of Portland, Maine, in 1885.[3]

Arcturus Zodiac Conrad had a name for the ages and a bearing for the pulpit. He first pastored at the historic Old South Congregational Church in Worcester, Massachusetts, and exhausted himself from his prodigious efforts. Park Street called him in 1905 despite his health problems. The church sought a minister who would capitalize on its potential and make good on its legacy. Over the course of almost one hundred years of existence, Park Street had championed a fiery brand of Trinitarian orthodoxy. Pastors of eminent background like Edward Dorr Griffin, Sereno Edwards Dwight (great-grandson of Jonathan Edwards), and Edward Beecher all ministered at the church. But Park Street's nineteenth-century history was embattled, as much a story of survival in the face of the spread of Unitarianism and irreligion as of growth. All this changed when Conrad became its pastor.

Those who received a letter from the pastor later in life encountered the full force of the man. His personal stationery listed both his degrees and a number of his published works: "A Z Conrad Ph.D., D.D. Author of: *The Gospel for an Age of Thought, Jesus Christ at the Crossroads, Comrades of the Carpenter, Secret of the Life Sublime, Radiant Religion, The Seven Finalities of Faith, You Must Go Right On.*"[4] On November 6, 1905, Conrad officially began his work at Park Street.[5] Conrad's era coincided with a historic season. Not long after he assumed full responsibility for the church, Park Street celebrated its centennial in 1909. In his remarks in the church's official commemorative literature, the minister sounded a bold note regarding the church's health: "Three years have passed. Morning congregations have more than doubled. Evening audiences have quadrupled. *The tide has turned.* A hundred encouraging features attend our work."[6] Conrad concluded the point with a prognostic flourish: "Standing on the threshold of the second century, with a hundred years of testimony as to the unfailing goodness of God, and the certainty that divine wisdom will be vouchsafed as required, he is neither audacious nor presumptuous who predicts a larger and greater contribution from Park Street Church in the interests of the kingdom of Jesus Christ through the coming century than has been witnessed in the past hundred years."[7]

Conrad's prediction proved better than he knew. His successor would be among the most respected ministers of the twentieth century. But Conrad was no retiring flower himself. After struggling to find the right minister for decades, the church had finally found a pastor whose constitution, intellect, and ambition matched its identity.

The new minister was loaded for bear in his new context. Soon after Conrad came to Brimstone Corner, as Park Street was then called, he took up a slate of activities. Conrad soon became president of the Florence Crittenton League of Compassion, the Home for Deaf Mutes, Aged or Blind, and the Evangelical Alliance of Boston. He was made a director of the New England Sabbath Protective League and served as vice-president of the Bible Club of Boston.[8]

These associations mattered to Conrad, but revival was in the air in 1909, and Conrad wanted it to visit Boston. In 1909, he led a citywide revival that featured the preaching of J. Wilbur Chapman, a prominent revivalist of this period, and that caused hundreds to profess Christian faith. All 160 participating churches reported increases in membership at the campaign's close. Several years later, Conrad led another citywide revival that featured the preaching of Billy Sunday. Large numbers of professions resulted from this event as well.[9]

No church benefited more from these undertakings than Park Street. Conrad quickly acquired a reputation as a preacher of "didactic, expository sermons."[10] He preached twice on Sunday: morning services for Christians and evangelistic messages in the evening, a format the church had followed for years and that it would continue to follow for many more. The church's reputation for stirring oratory drove its expanding membership. Margaret Bendroth summarizes Conrad's impact on the congregation's numbers: "Under Conrad's aggressive leadership, the congregation began to grow quickly. From 348 members in 1905, it nearly doubled by 1910, and by 1916 had passed one thousand."[11] By the 1930s, the church numbered over eighteen hundred members.

The Park Street pulpit became known for a no-compromise, no-holds-barred conservatism. Sounding something like Sunday, Conrad assailed modernism: "The adulterated, eviscerated, emasculated gospel of modernism blasts everything it touches. Avoid it as you would a pestilence."[12] Later in his pastorate, after president Franklin Delano Roosevelt inaugurated his New Deal, Conrad called it "socialistic and dictatorial."[13] Similar statements regularly issued from Park Street. Conrad clearly felt that his pulpit allowed him the leash to speak not only on spiritual matters but also on political and cultural ones. Park Street's decision to air Conrad's sermons and a weekly radio program on area stations only increased his influence as a public intellectual.[14] His bold manner of leadership helped attract the city's business class. Park Street tapped a young law school dean named Gleason L. Archer Sr. to head up a class for men in 1914. Hundreds of young men flocked to the class.[15] Similar efforts to reach young women and college students drew large numbers.

As the Roaring Twenties gave way to the Great Depression of the 1930s, Conrad began to weaken. Word traveled throughout the evangelical network and reached Machen. While Machen was intriguing to have Ockenga called to Boston, he left his charge without assurance of the future, noting that he was "extremely fearful as to the kind of pastor that they may get for that church." He ruminated out loud about Ockenga's prospects in the letter, noting that were he "going to see Dr. Conrad personally, I could in a very tactful and noncommittal way bring the matter up, since he was good about consulting me last year."[16]

Point Breeze was by now an unmediated success story. The church grew even as it cleaned up its inflated membership rolls through a concerted purge. The Sunday school, essentially the evangelistic program of the congregation, had grown to more than four hundred people.[17] Ockenga added a sixty-voice choir and retired the mortgage, all in the midst of the greatest economic depression in American history.[18] When Park Street reached out to Machen and Macartney for recommendations for possible successors to the ailing Conrad in February 1934, both men endorsed Ockenga.[19] The church then began a lengthy courtship of the young preacher, inviting him to preach no less than seven times between 1934 and 1936.

There soon was little doubt that Ockenga was the man for the future job. By January 21, 1935, Ockenga wrote to Machen that "Dr. Conrad is in correspondence with me and is thinking of a Co-Pastorate in a year or so depending on his health (confidential—things may change)."[20] Things did not change. On August 27, 1936, Park Street extended a unanimous call to Ockenga to serve as co-pastor with Conrad. In a round of interviews with the General Committee of the church, Ockenga affirmed his assent to the church's confession and the Westminster Confession of Faith, which Park Street had adopted as its broader doctrinal platform.[21] The young man raised in nominal Methodist circles, converted at a Keswick-flavored gathering in high school, trained at pious Taylor in the American heartland, and schooled at cosmopolitan Princeton and upstart Westminster had come full circle.

Ockenga was now the inheritor of the Park Street mantle that Conrad had done so much to enhance. He was the appointed herald of New England's best-known pulpit, itself associated firmly with confessional Reformed theology. Ockenga fit the part. Tall, lean, full of confidence and promise, and looking like the young executives he would soon cultivate for his institutional projects, he had a secretary, two months of vacation per year, and an annual salary of six thousand dollars. He settled into his work at the booming church, ready to learn from his fellow pastor.

Almost immediately, Conrad's health failed. On January 22, 1937, he passed away.[22] Just a few thousand feet from the famous Massachusetts State House, Park Street called for a pastor equipped for ideological debate and geared toward a leadership position in the great intellectual conflicts of the day. Ockenga himself said as much in 1941 when the *Boston Herald* profiled him. Ockenga declared to his interviewer that he "would rather live in Boston than in any part of the United States of America or of the world. Boston challenges me to do my best. I also feel that other systems of thought which have their centers in Boston and which compete with the system of thought which I advocate are a profound challenge to my intellect and my ability." He closed his remarks with a personal mission statement: "I preach and serve Christ first, last and always."[23]

From his earliest days in Boston, Ockenga found the city's intellectual climate thrilling. He did not shrink away from the "profound challenge" to his "intellect" that ministry in Boston offered. He embraced it and sought to be a pulpiteer who could reach the skeptical masses, the highly educated world-changers of Boston. The early years of Ockenga's pastorate show this in abundance.

Ockenga not only exposited the text at Park Street; he exegeted the culture. In a sermon titled "The Rebellion of Man Against God's Sovereignty" from Psalm 2:1, "Why do the heathen rage, and the people imagine a vain thing?" (KJV), the pastor declared his theological premise: "We may be sure that God lives and that He rules the universe." He then explored a cultural reference: "When Victor Hugo, meditating on the plain Sedan where Germany crushed France in 1870, said, 'In the terrible shadows I saw thee, O thou invisible one,' he was recording the providence of God in history. God has not only decreed but His decrees are unchangeable."[24] Ockenga's quotation of Hugo signaled to his audience that he spoke their cultural language and had heard the great questions raised by influential thinkers and artists. This was not imagined literary fluency. Ockenga read voraciously and genuinely exulted in the life of the mind. In an age in which evangelical preaching was known for being anticulture, Ockenga plundered the Egyptians—or in this case the French—to make his points.

Ockenga sounded similar notes in his sermon titled "Athens Looks to Jerusalem" based on John 12:21. In this message, the pastor considered the question posed by the early church father Tertullian, "What hath Athens to do with Jerusalem?" Ockenga suggested that the truth the philosophers sought was found in Jesus. He set the table for his main point by walking his people through the intellectual life of ancient Athens: "Athens became the center of our art treausres [sic], beauty and thought for the civilized world. Its Acropolis graced with the Parthenon, Erectheum, the Temple of Winged Victory, the Propylea was unequaled in any other center." Ockenga referenced the demise of Socrates as he continued: "Surrounding it were the Pynx where oratory and debates occurred and under which were the prison which must have contained Socrates before he drank the hemlock."[25] Instead of voicing distaste for the high culture of Athens, Ockenga celebrated it. He clearly found himself at home in such a place.

Ockenga enunciated his affection for Boston, the "Athens of America," in a striking 1950 sermon titled "Boston at the Crossroads." "[W]hen you consider the educational opportunities of this area," he mused, "we have more degree-granting colleges and universities in Massachusetts than we have in any other State of the Union and sixty per cent of them are concentrated right here in Boston." He relished this culture: "Go down the Charles River. You will see also the greatest technical Institution of learning in the whole world. You will see the greatest private university in America. You will see likewise one of the greatest City universities that we have in America." All this academic presence added up to tremendous intellectual capital— and tremendous capacity for evangelical influence. Some might have found this context unnerving; Ockenga found it enlivening. He had been called to the modern Athens, and though he had opportunities aplenty to leave it to be a pastor elsewhere, he never could.[26]

Ockenga loved also the orthodox tradition of the New England past. In a sermon titled "Jonathan Edwards and New England or the Apologetic of Protestantism," based on John 3:16 and Romans 9:16, he traced the life of New England's most famous preacher. As Ockenga walked his audience through Edwards' core convictions, he made the case for a fresh apologetic that married mind and heart. "Toward the end of his student life," Ockenga declaimed, "the conviction grew upon him that he ought to enter the ministry. It was attended by the acceptance of the truth of predestination and of the sovereignty of God. As the flower opens to the morning rays' [sic] of the sun, so Edwards heart [sic] warmed to this doctrine."

As Ockenga read him, Edwards was "a lover of logical thoroughness" whose view of predestination was "the most thoroughly logical doctrine in the theological field." Yet this did not mean that Edwards was a rationalist: "Edwards had no sudden or emotional conversion. It was the result of the thought processes of his mind, but it was attended and followed by remarkable personal experiences of God, so much so that Woodbridge Riley calls him a mystic."[27] Ockenga's conception of Edwards' conversion speaks volumes about his intellectual approach. For a university crowd, Ockenga emphasized that the Northampton pastor "was a lover of logical thoroughness." Predestination did not threaten the limits of the rational mind but was in fact "the most thoroughly logical doctrine" in all of theology, given a fundamental belief in the existence of God. Ockenga propounded the case that Christianity accords elegantly with, and does no violence to, the rational mind.

This was tough stuff for a New England crowd familiar with Emerson's over-soul and William James's pragmatism. But Ockenga did not shy away from identifying himself—and his pulpit—with Calvinism, which many years prior had shaped the New England mind. "Whatever we may think of Calvinism," he intoned, "it has produced more rugged, upright, courageous characters than any other system." Should one "[l]ook back in the history of New England and think of its intellectual lights and its leading characters of which we Americans are justly proud," one would discover "the product of three centuries of Calvinism, of strict adherence to the Bible teaching concerning the nature of man, the sovereignty of God and the need of a true regeneration in life."[28] Machen's tutelage was not lost on young Ockenga. His was a Calvinist pulpit. In his three-fold description of the system—"rugged, upright, and courageous"—we might hear echoes of what he believed he needed to be in his context.

The Ockengan pulpit was a lively one. One week Park Street members heard a thoroughgoing exposition of the glories of New England Calvinism. The next Sunday they listened to a homiletical discourse on the cultural richness of the Greco-Roman world. Later, they heard a detailed breakdown of the second blessing of the Spirit. Here we see how Ockenga resisted the strict doctrinal profile of his Presbyterian pedagogues. In a message titled "The Second Blessing, Sanctification and Holiness," preached on Luke 24:49, 1 Thessalonians 4:3, and Hebrews 12:14, Ockenga linked the pursuit of personal holiness to the pursuit of the second blessing. He defined himself carefully: "Thus the second blessing is not a second coming of the Holy Spirit upon the believer."[29]

He then suggested that "[a]ny second blessing of which we might speak, then, must be confined entirely to the act of consecration on the part of a believer with the resultant Divine response in filling the believer with the Holy Spirit." In Ockenga's calculation, the "act of consecration" initiated the experience, given by God, of the Spirit's "filling." This was the view popularized in the mid-nineteenth century by Phoebe Palmer. Palmer's views found a considerable audience in the American Holiness movement.[30] Her influence reached some surprising places, not least among them the sober Calvinist sanctuary just off of Boston Common.

Ockenga did not confine himself to theological, spiritual, and philosophical topics. He ranged in the political as well, offering his adherents generally conservative political commentary on an array of matters. In some cases, he preached directly political messages. The 1939 sermon "God Save America," based on Proverbs 29:18, called Americans to own their exceptionalism in the postwar world: "Ethiopia, Spain and China have been carved up. Poland is now invaded by a Blitz Krieg [sic]. France has been reduced to a second rate power dependent on England for its diplomacy." Ockenga's assessment of the state of European affairs was dire, but not without basis in fact. "Britain's influence," he continued, "has been disintegrating in the Far East under Japan, in the Mediterranean under Italy, and in Europe at the hands of Hitler."

In this global crisis, Ockenga posed a series of portentous questions for his American audience: "Is America to be the last stand of civilization, a repository for western civilization? Are we alone to emerge from this holocaust able to meet world communism unafraid? Are we then fulfilling our Divine mission?"[31] The passage is noteworthy for its mingling of political and spiritual salvation. America not only was "a repository for western civilization" but also had a "Divine mission" to fulfill. The nation could fill this geopolitical messianic role, but only if it adhered to a righteous moral and spiritual course. Ockenga's moral vision—and pulpit commentary—extended far beyond the bounds of his own congregation.[32]

A confident and convinced preacher like Ockenga could not avoid courting controversy over the course of his ministry, and he did not. The fires of contention rarely waxed hotter than when in 1957 Ockenga preached a message at the National Association of Evangelicals meeting advocating a gradualist approach to the then-vexing question of racial integration.[33] He offered pastoral counsel on various dimensions of the issue, noting that "[t]here is nothing Biblically, nothing morally, nothing legally against it but it is not wise, that is all, for expediency's sake because it is selfish."[34]

What Ockenga offered as prudence others read as provocation, and with some justification. This is not to say that Ockenga believed segregation was just; he did not. He believed, though, that desegregration came with its own set of societal troubles.[35] For example, Ockenga identified the wrongs done "white people in the South" during Reconstruction. In 1964, Ockenga sounded a similar note, preaching a message at his church titled "The Christian Faces Segregation and Other Social Problems" based on James 2:1.[36] Ockenga suggested that protestors of segregation should not break the law even as he argued that all public facilities and churches should be integrated, but not by force: "If we break the law by forcing the situation we are going to encourage the extremist groups. We ought to be careful what we do." Though each of these affairs drew national media attention, it does not appear that such coverage endured beyond the events in question.

It is difficult, in sum, to fit Ockenga into a strict proclamatory profile. He preached old-style Calvinism; he expounded the glories of aesthetic culture; he called for the infilling of the second blessing; he threw down the political gauntlet. All of these instincts characterized the Park Street pulpit during his tenure. This does not obscure the reality that the body of Ockenga's sermonic work was an unapologetically high-minded blend of exegesis, theology, philosophy, cultural commentary, and pulpit evangelism.[37] The pastor was not merely an expositor of a text in Ockenga's eyes. The pastor was a pedagogue, an exegete, a dogmatic philosopher, an intellectual showman, a rational mystic. He provided leadership of a moral, philosophical, and intellectual kind to the Christian community through his preaching.

Preaching was all-consuming and all-important for Ockenga. Reflecting on his pastoral legacy toward the close of his life, Ockenga said that "[i]f you have a strong pulpit ministry, you're going to have a strong church, no matter if everything else is lacking."[38] He conceived of the pastor as a pastor-teacher. "The pastor-teacher," he said in an interview with *Christianity Today* late in his life, "is the essence of the pastor-preacher. A man can't preach two or three times a week without teaching. He has to have content.. . .This was not running comment—I preached 30 or 40 sermons on a book of Scripture."

He devoted countless hours to this task and kept up a demanding reading and research schedule for himself. Kenneth Kantzer, a doctoral student in Boston during the 1940s, told a revealing story about Ockenga in 1981: "One of the secrets of Ockenga's success as a pastor and church leader was his thorough preparation for everything he did. He prepared his sermons from the Greek text and has continued to study his Greek Testament throughout his ministry." This exegetical style gained the respect of the leading academic lights of Boston, as did Ockenga's polished delivery. He wrote out every word of his sermons but committed them to memory before stepping into the church's elevated pulpit and delivering them flawlessly, with the occasional rhetorical flourish. This he did four times a week for thirty-three years.

The core of Ockenga's preaching was a spiritual or theological topic derived, in many places, from one or two short biblical passages. In spots, the Boston pastor preached exegetically, working through a book. Most often—in slight disjunction from his remarks to *Christianity Today*—he grouped his sermons in terms of a common spiritual or theological theme taken directly from a passage of Scripture. The backbone of Ockenga's ministry was preaching, and the marrow of his preaching was stout theological and doctrinal content.[39]

Like praying, dying, and the act of preaching, Ockenga was ready to *discuss* preaching at a moment's notice. Randall Frame remembered an impromptu discussion that transformed his own pulpit work:

> While serving as Dr. Ockenga's student assistant at Park Street in 1937, I made my way to his tower study after a Sunday morning worship service. Intrigued by his sermon content and flawless delivery, I asked, "Dr. Ockenga, could you take time to explain to me your method of sermon preparation and delivery?" Without hesitation, while he showered and dressed, he launched into a homiletical lecture and study that surpassed all the college, seminary, and graduate speech courses I ever had. It revolutionized my own preaching style. It challenged me to prayerful subject selection, thorough biblical research and preparation, careful word-for-word manuscript writing, detailed and comprehensive sermon outlining, memorization of the sermon outline, and utter dependence upon the Holy Spirit for preaching without notes.[40]

Ockenga approached the task of preaching with zeal. He was no mere preacher, but a homiletical athlete. Week by week for thirty-two years, Ockenga labored to craft a thoughtful sermon that would stimulate his audience and move them to reflection and action.[41] This work, in his view, was the penultimate responsibility of his calling.[42] Though preaching was not treated by all of Ockenga's contemporaries in the prewar years as such an expressly intellectual enterprise, in Ockenga's mind the pastor was nothing if not an instructor of his congregation.

At times, Ockenga's original sermonic method led him, in a

literal sense, to some unexpected conclusions. Pastor Timothy Keller of Redeemer Presbyterian Church in Manhattan was a student at Gordon-Conwell during Ockenga's later years as president. Decades later, he recalled a fiery sermon of Ockenga's. In the course of his forceful delivery, he knocked a cup of water over, spraying the first row of his audience.[43] To Keller's surprise, Ockenga did not miss a beat but continued preaching as if nothing had happened. Gordon Hugenberger, current pastor of Park Street, later remembered a similar homiletical feat. While training for ministry, Hugenberger heard Ockenga preach a homily in which he suddenly forgot which sermon he was working through. Without missing a beat, and without the congregation noticing, Ockenga switched to an entirely different message and proceeded to deliver it flawlessly.[44] Here was aptitude in the task of preaching: despite his forgetfulness, the veteran pastor could deliver not one but *two* messages without notes.

A human whirlwind like Ockenga could not contain his awakening efforts to Sunday morning, however. He sought revival beyond the walls of the church with a zeal that stood out even to the boldest preachers of his day. Billy Graham was once traveling through Boston and had occasion to stop by Park Street and call on Ockenga. It was an unplanned visit, and Graham expected to find the pastor working on administrative matters or preparing one of his homilies. Years later, Graham recalled his surprise at finding Ockenga underneath his rug: "One day, I called on him in his office at Park Street Church—entering his office unexpectedly I could hear him but not see him. He was audibly praying through tears, beseeching the Lord. I found him under a throw rug that he had placed on himself in creating his private prayer room. Ockenga was a mighty man of God."[45]

Ockenga's zest for spiritual revival led him to enthusiastic partnership with Graham. In 1949, Graham's star was on the rise. The evangelist had, earlier in the decade, become the most-traveled civilian passenger of American Airlines. Graham's star would soon rise to still greater heights, though, as newspaper magnate William R.

Hearst would reportedly instruct his staff to "puff Graham" following the remarkable response to the evangelist's September 1949 Los Angeles crusade.

Ockenga had already seen Graham's unusual ability as an evangelist and invited him to Boston to preach evangelistically. Graham later remembered Ockenga's own facility as an evangelist during his visit: "On New Year's Eve, 1949, I had been invited to preach at Mechanics Hall in Boston. That night an overflow crowd gathered, prompting Dr. Ockenga to reserve the hall for the next afternoon." Graham became nervous in the face of the MIT-heavy audience. Ockenga was not ruffled, according to Graham: "Seeing the crowds, Dr. Ockenga intervened again and encouraged a continuation of the meetings for several more days in a variety of places including Park Street Church, Mechanics Hall and other venues culminating in a closing service at Boston Gardens. He was always an encouragement to me."[46] The impression Ockenga made on Graham from these and other experiences is itself noteworthy. Graham did not mince words in his summary of his friend: "I never met a man among evangelicals who could compare to the mighty intellect and spiritual development of Harold John Ockenga."[47]

The pastor sought revival constantly during his pastoral tenure. But he had to balance this interest with many other tasks native to pastoral leadership of a large urban congregation. He maintained a demanding schedule at the church, providing direction and tutoring to a hundred different initiatives.[48] One of his secretaries, Mary C. MacKenzie, sketched a portrait of a typical day in the life of the "whirlwind" pastor:

> Take today, for instance. This morning he recorded sermons at radio station WHDH and then returned to the church at 11:30 to attack a great sheaf of correspondence. After reading letters and dictating answers, commenting on questions concerning church work, or notes left for his attention, he sat down for a talk with Mr. Toms over church business. At 12:15 he dashed off to Rotary and to lunch,

returning at 1:30 to dictate more correspondence. This was interrupted by a half-hour long-distance call from Billy Graham. Soon afterward there was another ringing phone and another long-distance call, this time an EMERGENCY! Would he please fill an important speaking engagement Friday?[49]

In the midst of this whirlwind of activity, Ockenga maintained a demeanor of enviable equipoise. He did not walk during the day but powered through it, though with perfect posture, a winning smile, and intense eyes that fix upon the viewer even now, thirty years after his going hence.

Years after the fact, Gordon-Conwell Theological Seminary professor Ken Swetland remembered Ockenga's penchant for economizing his workday. As a promising young student at Gordon Divinity School, Swetland was deeply honored when asked to escort Ockenga from downtown Boston to South Hamilton, Massachusetts, site of the divinity school. He recalled later his excitement at some precious personal time with the Park Street pastor. When he pulled up to the church building, however, his expectations quickly changed: "He got into his seat, nodded to me, and then took a book out of his briefcase. For the next hour, he read without saying a word to me." Swetland dropped Ockenga off at his meeting, hoping to talk with him on the return trip. When Ockenga got in the car, he took out his book, began reading, and did not say another word.[50] The experience might have been disillusioning to some; Swetland recalled it with a laugh. He later joined the GCTS faculty under Ockenga.

One senses the tensions of such a productive life as Ockenga's in a piece written by Audrey Ockenga in 1966 in the *Park Street Spire*, the church's magazine. This was a rare public word from Ockenga's wife, and it was remarkably candid. Audrey Ockenga shared with the magazine's readers that "[o]ur life was so wrapped up in Park Street that our children's lives, too, were conditioned and regulated by it. Their Daddy was away much of the time and I fell into the category of church widow. . . . Harold would leave after breakfast when he was

not travelling and, most days, would not return until late at night."
Nevertheless, Audrey concluded that "[l]iving with Harold has been
the crown of life. To be a co-laborer with him has been pure joy. I am
the only one who knows what an exacting schedule he keeps, how
great is his weariness, and how deep his selfless devotion to the work
of Christ. Through it all he keeps great equanimity of spirit. His family salutes him at this milestone of his life."[51]

Audrey Ockenga's task was not an enviable one. A major part of
life with Ockenga, whether personally or ecclesially, was keeping up
with his many interests. Few of his early initiatives were more ambitious than Park Street's Boston School of the Bible, however. Ockenga
established the school in 1944 even as he entered his third and final
year as president of the National Association of Evangelicals and discharged a number of tasks as pastor of the thriving church. An early
document titled "Boston Bible School" spelled out the rationale for
the school: "The layman is playing an increasingly important role in
the life of our churches. To do this effectively he needs training." This
could be accomplished by the founding of a school for laypeople: "The
answer is clearly a school for lay service to a great many churches.
This assures a more adequate training for a greater number, with a
great saving in money and effort."[52]

The first course offered the following courses to the interested
student: the Pauline Epistles, the Synoptic Gospels, John, Apostolic
History, Old and New Testament Criticism, the Major and Minor
Prophets, and Archaeology and the Bible. The school began with a
bang. In Ockenga's pastor's report to the church on January 11, 1944,
he noted that "the throng of 475 registered students at the Evening
School of the Bible necessitates more space. We look forward to many
years of wide influence by means of this school planned by your pastor and brought into existence jointly by Park Street Church and
Providence Bible Institute."[53] Ockenga's remarks announced that Park
Street would devote its basement to the school, a change of policy. To
make ends meet, the church had for over half a century rented out its

basement for "commercial use." The Evening School, however, had drawn 475 students before it even opened its doors. It was a runaway success.

Working closely with Terrelle Crum of the Providence Bible Institute, Ockenga tested and tweaked his plans for the school. From thin air, he had founded a training institute that outnumbered most seminaries. The school drew attendees from all over the surrounding area. Gleason L. Archer Jr., the church's bright young assistant minister, noted at the church's annual meeting in January 1946 that the school's "students come from over a hundred different churches in Greater Boston, many of which are Liberal or Modernist Churches, and some of these students hear the true gospel for the first time in our class sessions."[54]

The school soon boasted a student body that rivaled that of many Bible colleges and Christian schools, though it had no full-time administrator. Ockenga handed off many of the administrative duties to his protégé.[55] Though Archer served ably and the school had promise, Ockenga soon grew frustrated with the level of instruction provided by the program. He wrote to Terrelle Crum that "[o]ur lectures and discussion do not have the atmosphere of mental awareness and true educational value that secular students find required of them in economics and technology, and this is to my mind a serious—and an unnecessary—failing."[56] Ockenga was glad that believers from 150 churches attended the school. But almost as soon as it was launched, the initiative befuddled him.

The people he cared for needed a certain "mental awareness" that this and other efforts could not give them. Ockenga hungered for a more ambitious work, one that would represent a fuller embodiment of his vision of an enlightened Christian populace able to engage theology, philosophy, and exegesis at the highest levels. The Boston School of the Bible was in his view a worthy effort, but it seems clear from the pastor's frustrated writings that the evening school did not meet his lofty goals.

The pastor would not have to wait long to discharge his ambitions, however. A new movement was soon to break. As Ockenga discovered in the 1940s, a number of brilliant young evangelicals possessing the ability and ambition to begin a far more holistic work than the School of the Bible were journeying, without a formal call or overarching strategy, to Boston to gain elite academic training. The grand scheme Ockenga desired to implement would soon take shape. The evangelical movement would never be the same.

CHAPTER 3

THREE MYSTICS, THREE SKEPTICS, AND THREE EVANGELICALS

Trial by Fire at Harvard

As he made his way across America and around the world, evangelist Billy Sunday punched the air, stamped his feet, and wept with great pathos. He was a consummate performer and the world's most prolific evangelist, able in his day to persuade his countrymen to amend the US Constitution and ban alcohol. On occasion, to punctuate his points, Sunday would dash across his platform and break into a slide into an invisible home plate. One moment, he roared against sin. The next, he brought the audience to tears by telling stories about mothers whose hearts were crushed by their alcoholic sons. If Sunday were not real and proven so by historical documentation, we might think a journalist had dreamed him up as a foil.

He was no imaginary figure, though. Formerly the fastest man in baseball, Sunday was in his day an evangelical kingmaker, possessing the ability to mold the movement. He built a mansion in Winona Lake, Indiana, traveled the world with his wife "Ma" Sunday, and brought in hundreds of thousands of dollars from his revivals. Everywhere he went, he preached the new birth, emphasizing the need of all his hearers, high-born or low, to follow Jesus. In many crusades respondents were literally to do so. Responding in faith to Sunday's gospel message meant walking down the sawdust aisles of a "tabernacle" usually built for the revival. His was a down-home fundamentalism, a plain-and-simple biblicism, and he resisted what he saw as the over-thinking of the faith common to some of his more scholarly peers: "I don't know any more about *theology* than a *jack-rabbit* does about ping-pong," he fulminated, "but I'm on the way to glory."[1] That, in a nutshell, was Sunday's approach to doctrine.

This quotation is not merely an epigram. It captures the mindset of many fundamentalists and conservative Protestants of Sunday's period. For these believers, salvation through Jesus Christ was the most important truth in the eyes of all evangelicals. Sometimes, in fact, it could seem like it was the *only* important truth. Sunday and his followers took pride in not getting lost in the thickets of higher criticism and the swamps of systematic theology. Better to keep oneself unstained by the world, the flesh, and the academy.[2]

Harold John Ockenga had very different views about the life of the mind. But Ockenga was not alone in this conviction. In the midst of the fundamentalist heyday, a growing contingent of young Christians rejected the kind of thinking epitomized by Sunday's epigram. Where many Christians turned away from the higher academy in the wake of several cataclysmic cultural defeats and focused on invigorating their own institutions and movements, a small core of bright young evangelicals, introduced here as the *Cambridge evangelicals*, attempted to re-enter secular schools for the purpose of training themselves to think at the highest levels and to earn elite credentials. They thus represent a profound counter-move to the anti-intellectualism of their peers. Before we delve into their story, we examine the disruptive cultural moment in which they grew up.

The first third of the twentieth century was fraught with major cultural defeats for fundamentalists and conservative Christians.

In addition to the Presbyterian and Northern Baptist controversies, evangelicals suffered several staggering losses in the cultural arena in this era. The two most damaging setbacks were the Scopes Trial in 1925 and the repeal of Prohibition in 1933. The Scopes Trial set in stone fundamentalism's intellectually backward reputation.[3] The acrid exchanges between defense attorney Clarence Darrow and star prosecution witness William Jennings Bryan were the heart of the problem.[4]

Though Bryan was a former secretary of state, he withered under Darrow's clever questioning. Lacking sophisticated answers, Bryan's "laudable simple faith became laughable crude belief when applied to Jonah's whale, Noah's flood, and Adam's rib."[5] The sharp pen of critic and reporter H. L. Mencken of the *Baltimore Sun* only heaped up more scorn for Bryan in the eyes of many elite Americans. At the trial's close, he pronounced Bryan a "a poor clod...full of an almost pathological hatred of all learning, all human dignity, all beauty, all fine and noble things. He was a peasant come home to the dung-pile. Imagine a gentleman, and you have imagined everything he was not."[6] Mencken's forceful indictment of Bryan exerted lasting influence on the American psyche, helping at some level to discredit conservative Christians on intellectual grounds.[7]

Fundamentalists and their peers faced a second major cultural defeat when Prohibition was repealed in 1933. Sunday's preaching had figured prominently in the passing of the eighteenth amendment to the US Constitution. Officers made more than five hundred thousand arrests for violations of this law.[8] Nonetheless, enforcement of the ban grew nearly impossible, and a wave broke out across the nation to repeal the amendment. When this happened, in December 1933, Sunday and many of his fundamentalist supporters were crestfallen. The evangelist interpreted the events as a sign that judgment had grown closer, and he suffered a heart attack a few months later. The symbolism of the blow seemed all too obvious: the fundamentalist cause, like its leader, was stricken.[9]

In concert with the defeats suffered in the fundamentalist-modernist controversy, doctrinally conservative Christians retreated in large numbers from the popular culture and focused on building their own institutions. It is simplistic to conclude that the fundamentalists only retreated, however. They were hastened toward the retreat by the machinations of their skeptical counterparts. This was particularly true in higher education, where in Joel Carpenter's view, denominational colleges followed "the universities' lead in divorcing theological thought from other forms of learning."[10] This led in the estimation of many Christians to "the waning of evangelical piety, moral constraints, and religious idealism on these campuses."[11] The climate of many formerly evangelical colleges and universities, characterized by both a more progressive educational stance and a relaxed ethical perspective, alarmed many Christian gatekeepers.

If the Ivy League had turned its back on fundamentalists, they would create their own institutions. The *ne plus ultra* of this entrepreneurial instinct was the Bible institute. According to Virginia Brereton, "Bible schools stood out. Probably more than fundamentalist colleges or seminaries, they became the educational standard bearers for the movement."[12] The Bible school focused on a curriculum revolving around study of the contents of the Bible, which they believed was the foundation and essence of education (per 2 Tim. 3:16).

The practical thrust of this emphasis meant that students took numerous classes dedicated to study of biblical books in English. Where many Christian schools had studied the Word in the original languages, working exegetically through passages, modern fundamentalist "Bible school teachers disparagingly referred to such an approach as the analysis of 'fragments' of Scripture." The pedagogical imperative in this system was that "the student ought to master the entire Bible before attempting to study its parts," in Brereton's summation.[13] The Bible school curriculum, intended to be traditional, was in truth progressive. The model was a new one and signaled that the Christian educational task centered in practical, readily accessible biblical study, not high-level philosophical and theological engagement with leading scholars and their ideas.

At the most elemental level, distrust of non-Christian thought reached such heights that it was considered out-of-bounds. Some in the fundamentalist movement had seen young people, particularly the more academically inclined, walk away from the faith after attending elite institutions. They had felt the sting of ridicule, and they wanted to shield their children from it. Education became more about safety than about exploration. Conservative leaders made the paradigm clear. John R. Rice, for decades a fundamentalist spokesperson, argued that "when the Wesleyan movement was red hot with fervor and the power of God, but mainly with poor and unlettered people, it was a mighty force for God, but when scholarship and riches and modernistic theology came in, then the Lord wrote Ichabod over the doors of the Methodist denomination."[14] In Rice's estimation, one shared by many peers, the lust for "scholarship" had poisoned the Methodist well. The implication was that once the people acquire a taste for learning, liberal theology cannot stay far behind. The two go hand-in-hand. Better to stay humble and "unlettered" and poor.

The desire to found truly Christian schools produced a veritable cornucopia of Bible schools in the 1920s and '30s. Like a galaxy springing into existence from nothing, doctrinally conservative Christians from a range of backgrounds created schools like the Simpson Bible Institute of Seattle; the Omaha Bible Institute; Cincinnati Bible College; the Harrisburg School of the Bible; Atlanta Christian College; Baltimore School of the Bible; Baptist Bible Seminary; the People's Bible School of Greensboro, New York; Bay Cities Bible Institute of Oakland; the Colorado School of the Bible in Denver; the Keystone School of the Bible in Pittsburgh; and the Akron Bible Institute.[15] These and dozens of other institutes and colleges joined with established schools like the Moody Bible Institute and Wheaton College to constitute a key part of the institutional core of fundamentalism. In the midst of a recession of sorts, the fundamentalists and conservative Christians had embarked on a building campaign of historic proportions.

Fundamentalists shared a distinct understanding of the purpose of education. Michael Hamilton has suggested that "[f]undamentalists valued college for many of the same reasons as did other Americans. In the twentieth century, college came to be seen as an essential capstone to a person's general education, serving either as a finishing school, a launching pad for a profession, or as a preparation for further professional training."[16] Conservative Protestants were not alone, in other words, in wanting training that suited a future career. Though they distrusted the secular academy, they continued to found institutions at a blistering pace, albeit institutions with a more circumscribed educational ministry than other academic models.

These nuances notwithstanding, it is easy in retrospect to chide the fundamentalist form of college. Those both within and without the evangelical movement have recognized the difficulties Christians have faced in sustaining colleges and universities that are both academically excellent and confessionally faithful. The fundamentalists were not alone in seeking to preserve the faith of their students while providing them with academic uplift; Cotton Mather and Timothy Dwight encountered this challenge long before Rice sounded a warning. In some senses, this is the perennial question for Christians: how to sustain educational institutions, birthed in promise, that seek both academic excellence and heartfelt spirituality.

The neo-evangelicals, like the fundamentalists before them, would provide their own attempt at an answer. They would seek to learn from fundamentalism, seen from their vantage point as a marginalized, perhaps insecure, but by no means defeated movement. In an age of tremendous economic challenges, it was clear to many that the fundamentalists built an underground empire. But as we will see, a host of young evangelical minds were not satisfied with a subterranean presence. They wanted to go above ground. They came to Boston to attempt just that.

In the early 1940s, a group of doctrinally conservative students came to Boston to study, primarily, at Harvard. Included in this group were Samuel Schultz, Kenneth Kantzer, Merrill Tenney, John Gerstner, Burton Goddard, Roger Nicole, Terelle Crum, Edward John Carnell, Gleason Archer, George Eldon Ladd, Paul King Jewett, George Turner, J. Harold Greenlee, Jack P. Lewis, Lemoine Lewis, Lloyd Dean, and Glenn Barker. Carl F. H. Henry was also in Boston during this time, working on his doctorate at Boston University.[17] Historian Rudolph Nelson labeled the students the "Harvard fundamentalists," a clever title but a potentially misleading one due to the fact that not all of the students were fundamentalists.[18] We might reclassify them as the Cambridge evangelicals.

The convergence of the Cambridge evangelicals is nothing less than remarkable. It was noticed at the highest levels of Harvard Divinity School (HDS) and was a genuine phenomenon in its day, for the average graduating class from all programs of the divinity school rarely exceeded twenty. This was a curious development in the eyes of the school's faculty; Kantzer noted years later that "[t]he professors at Harvard did not quite understand why there was this sudden invasion of fundamentalist students."[19] Precious few evangelicals had graduated from the school in previous years. Kantzer remembered only Walter Maier, a Lutheran evangelist, as a predecessor to the young scholars.[20]

The Cambridge evangelicals came to Harvard in a unique season. As America ramped up for its second major war in three decades, numbers flagged at the Divinity School, creating openings for students that Harvard would otherwise have rejected. The dean of the school, Willard R. Sperry, found the educational pedigree of the scholars lacking and showed no compunction about saying so.[21] According to one source, the situation at HDS grew so grave in the prewar period that "its faculty, students, and budget were a quarter to a fifth the size of competitors Yale, Chicago, and Union Theological Seminary."[22]

Harvard President James Conant expressed in confidence a wish to shut the school down entirely.[23] The school had fallen out of favor with the administration some time before due to its flagging enrollment. Charles William Eliot, the man who transformed the university into the world's preeminent research university, suggested early in his tenure that the school consisted of "three mystics, three skeptics, and three dyspeptics."[24] Had he made this comment in the 1940s, he might have added "three evangelicals" to the mix.

Harvard needed the Cambridge evangelicals as much as they needed Harvard. Once through the portal, the young scholars found the style of pedagogy amenable to their success. HDS professors in this period generally focused less on the theology of the biblical text and more on issues of textual historicity, language, and historiography. Though these instructors made clear their lack of interest in evangelical beliefs, they spoke publicly of their desire to be fair. Kantzer remembered a principal statement of his doctor-father, Johann Abraham Christophel Fanginger Auer: "You may believe the earth is flat if you wish, but you will have to know why other people, including me, do not. And you will have to explain intelligibly why you believe it to be flat. If you meet these standards, I will support you in your program towards the degree."[25]

In time, the evangelicals proved themselves and won the respect of professors like Henry J. Cadbury. Cadbury not only tolerated the students but seemed to enjoy the stimulation they provided in class discussion.[26] This method influenced the Cambridge evangelicals. Many of them had been exposed to the prevailing mode of fundamentalist education, which shied away from extensive engagement of nonevangelical sources. In later years at Wheaton and Trinity Evangelical Divinity School (TEDS), Kantzer practiced the method learned under his HDS professors, giving considerable attention in his systematic theology classes to neo-orthodox doctrine.[27] This example held true for many of the Cambridge evangelicals, who came to pride themselves on engaging scholars outside their own camp.

These bright evangelical doctoral students relished their time in

Boston, sitting at the feet of elite theologians and thinkers. They did not come to the city as a formal group, of course. But they did feel kinship and were aware in their own day of the strange nature of their convergence. Kantzer spoke to the sense among the Cambridge evangelicals of a "club," which was "thoroughly open and its meetings were always informal. Standing around in the intermission between classes, or on the way to the library, we would discuss the issues that had come up in class. Informal meetings took place in our homes where we honed our Christian world and life view." The club was strikingly ambitious, particularly given the climate of the era: "[W]e were convinced that we had the answers for which the world was waiting."[28] Some of the scholars had already met at the early gatherings of the National Association of Evangelicals, founded in 1942 with Ockenga as its first president. The NAE represented a new initiative among evangelicals to engage the great social issues of the day, cooperate across denominational lines, and stimulate fresh thinking on great ethical and spiritual matters.[29]

The foregoing provides a brief overview of the convergence of the Cambridge evangelicals in Boston. The personal narratives and correspondence of four members of this group offer a more expansive look into the unique intellectual program and bewildering experience of the young scholars. Fresh archival work in the papers of Kenneth Kantzer, Carl F. H. Henry, E. J. Carnell, and George Eldon Ladd details just how vibrant—and unusual—the intellectual vision of these future neo-evangelical leaders was.

Kenneth Kantzer grew up in Detroit, son to a factory worker. He attended Ashland College and later Ohio State University. While Kantzer grew up in church, he was not then a born-again Christian. He reminisced about his background late in life in a chapel sermon at TEDS, noting that in his boyhood congregation, the pastor was paid "to study the Bible, and to pray, and to prepare sermons. We paid him to be religious for all of us. He was to be good and very spiritual. The rest of us didn't need to pray. We didn't need to study our Bibles. We didn't need to bear witness to others. We paid the pastor—the minister—to do all those things."[30] Kantzer was a nominal Christian and was not particularly religious until he read C. S. Lewis in the midst of an intellectual crisis. His encounter with Lewis's *Mere Christianity* led to a total commitment to Christianity, and a recognition that he needed greater resources to "defend" the gospel.[31]

Kantzer found himself frustrated by the intellectual posture of fellow evangelicals. In this age, "American fundamentalism of the twenties and thirties failed to understand the culture in which it was seeking to minister. I say this with care, because present-day evangelicals have to be grateful for in [*sic*] their evangelical heritage." Kantzer later concluded that "a generation of fundamentalists walled themselves off from the very world their Biblical mandate had commanded them to serve."[32] Kantzer wanted to break from this mold. Graduating from Faith Theological Seminary in 1942 with a Bachelor of Divinity, Kantzer made his way to Harvard. There, with his fellow evangelicals, he "secured a deep appreciation for the disciplined life of a scholar, and the importance of scholarship if evangelicalism were to make its necessary impact upon our society."[33]

Kantzer's class notebooks at Harvard support his statements. In classes like Cadbury's New Testament Introduction and Auer's Systematic Theology, Kantzer demonstrated a thirst for learning and an impressive capacity for note-taking. Though he generally seems to have viewed his professors as authoritative, in places he clearly argued in the confines of his notebooks with his tutors. In Cadbury's lecture on Acts 2, the professor suggested that the Jews were not recognized in this period as a "political" reality (the "Jews" were "tribal," according to Cadbury). Kantzer labeled Cadbury's depiction of Judaism "Weak" in bold red pen.[34] Elsewhere the doctoral student argued not with his professor but with historic figures. In Auer's lecture on the church, he presented Martin Luther's view on the visible aspect of the church. Kantzer recorded Luther's position as follows:

A. Every community on earth if it is not to fall to pieces must have a bodily head, under the true head, which is Christ.

B. Inasmuch as all Christendom is one community on earth it must have a head, which is the pope.

Next to this statement, Kantzer, future head of a divinity school run by the Evangelical Free Church of America, wrote in red ink, "NO."[35] His note-taking restraint could not withstand the prospect of a non-Christic human head of the church.

At one point, Kantzer responded to a survey for Professor Hackett on the nature of knowledge. The questionnaire was mailed to a plethora of eminent theologians. In his response, Kantzer articulated his doctrine of the image of God as it related to humankind's ability to know truth. He argued logically for the existence of higher truth: "My ultimate unproved assumption is that there is such a thing as truth. By truth I mean congruency to the standard of actuality. I believe I have to assume this because it cannot be denied (Cf. Descartes)."[36] Kantzer further suggested that truth was "horizontally consistent" and "vertically" realistic, a view that Francis Schaeffer would popularize two decades later.

The challenging climate of Harvard forced Kantzer and his peers to voice such opinions in an environment that challenged them. This climate had a salutary effect on the Cambridge evangelicals. Kantzer later noted that prior evangelical thought had grown "isolated" from prevailing academic and cultural discussions. In his eyes, he and his peers set out to remedy this situation not merely by making contributions to their disciplines but by attempting no less ambitious a task than "an intellectual rehabilitation" of their movement. This testimony enhances our understanding of the aims of the Cambridge evangelicals and of their peers in this heady time. As Kantzer makes clear, he believed that the training afforded him and his peers in Boston had enabled them to master "the skills" necessary for an intellectual revolution.

Kenneth Kantzer was not alone in seeking to learn such intellectual jujitsu. Edward Carnell and Carl Henry had similar goals and shared with one another these prospects in an exchange of letters that stretches over their time at Boston University. Carnell and Henry had each graduated from Wheaton College—Carnell in 1941, Henry in 1938 (BA) and 1940 (MA). Henry was older than Carnell by five years and had already earned a doctorate from Northern Baptist Theological Seminary in 1942. He taught at Northern while studying at BU as a doctoral student in philosophy of religion, beginning his coursework in 1942.[37] Carnell graduated from Westminster Theological Seminary in 1944 and then embarked upon not one but two doctoral degrees while serving as pastor of the First Baptist Church of Marblehead, Massachusetts, before teaching at Gordon College in Wenham, Massachusetts, starting in 1946. This fact alone—that both Carnell and Henry earned two doctorates—tells us a great deal about the unusual academic ambitions of these two future neo-evangelicals.

Henry was in this period the more accomplished of the two. He wrote articles for the *Chicago Tribune*, was a professor at Northern, and had turned his dissertation into a book, *Successful Church Publicity*, before he was thirty years of age, an enviable feat. A tall, broad-shouldered man, Henry enjoyed both the pondering of great intellectual questions in the classroom and the staccato style of the smoke-filled newsroom. His writing, then and later, would at times represent a quixotic blend of the two: theological insight mediated through newspaper copy. E. J. Carnell was also an idiosyncratic figure. He wore thick glasses, slicked his hair back, and sported a three-piece suit in even scorching heat. In his letters, as in stimulating classroom settings, Carnell came alive. He was bumptious, insatiably curious, and rarely stepped back from his work.

Henry and Carnell had a shared mentor in Gordon Clark of Wheaton. Clark was a pugnacious though luminous teacher.[38] Some students resented both his Reformed conclusions and his demanding approach, which depended on extensive representation of the theology and philosophy of various schools of thought. Others found him an intellect of the first rank. Carnell and Henry belonged to the latter group. Like Machen with Ockenga, Clark encouraged these gifted young men to seek elite training and practice excellent, academically rigorous scholarship.[39]

In November 1943, Carnell wrote Henry to get his advice on graduate schools. Henry was then a professor at Northern Seminary, one of the schools that Carnell was considering for further study. Carnell, however, wished to go to a more prestigious divinity school. On November 20, 1943, he stated his reasons for desiring this preparation in a lengthy letter to his elder: "It seems that my heart is being convicted more and more daily in the matter of the training of our ministers. The reason why Modernism is spreading so rapidly is because of the large number of seminaries pledged to that philosophy." The solution was fairly simple: "As I reason, then, conversely Modernism could be reduced if more schools returned to the historic interpretation of the Word of God."[40]

Carnell offered an expansion of the problems facing evangelical seminaries, problems he wished to counter: "Modernism, Humanism, and Barthianism are three philosophies of life which are sweeping our seminaries. When they once have found home it is but a short time before higher criticism enters in all the Biblical departments." Carnell wanted to strike back at higher criticism.[41] Several months later, Carnell filled Henry in on his prospects. Writing on March 4, 1944, he said he had applied to Harvard Divinity School and the University of Pennsylvania. Carnell cracked his knuckles as he surveyed possible contributions to theological discourse: "You see, Doctor, I have almost dismissed the problem of Modernism. I battled with that in college under Clark, with great security in our position."[42] Though not unfamiliar to graduate students, Carnell's intellectual confidence is striking.

"Ed," as Henry called him, enrolled at Harvard Divinity School in 1944.[43] A year later, he wrote to Henry once more. He had begun teaching at Gordon in the summer of 1945 and had taken on several courses once the fall term began. On November 11, 1945, Carnell mentioned his coursework at Harvard and how it proceeded: "This week at Harvard I read a thesis before a seminary [*sic*] on the Epistemology of William James. This seminary group seemed satisfied with my interpretation. I consider it one more step on the stony path of knowledge." On February 12, 1946, he wrote again on stationery from the Gordon College of Theology and Missions. He would soon submit his resignation to the Marblehead church. He noted that he was "looking forward, by the way, to reading your book on the 'Remaking of the Modern Mind.' How you can turn out so much amazes me!"[44] The remark was uncharacteristically modest. In terms of literary production over the next few decades, the two scholars constituted in themselves a minor arms race.

Carnell wrote further of his Harvard classes, shedding light on the demanding curriculum he took on at the Divinity School, which included "(1) Metaphysics of Aristotle, (2) Later Dialogues of Plato, (3) Post-Reformation Protestant Thinking, (4) Philosophy of Contemporary Physics (audit only), and (5) Seminar on the Problem of Evil—taught by Nels Ferre, prof. of theology at Andover Newton." Carnell expressed a wish to offer up some critique of Ferre: "I am awaiting the last-named course with great eagerness for I feel the man is wide open to trenchant criticisms. He has some sort of a mixed up *agape* theory of the Christian revelation, the same old liberalism in a new wrapping."[45] Again, Carnell showed a strong desire to engage professors whose beliefs differed from his own. He wanted, in fact, to set them straight.

Henry sent Carnell a copy of an article on June 13, 1946, that was to be "part of a series to be printed in book from under the captaion [*sic*] of THE UNEASY CONSCIENCE OF MODERN FUNDAMENTALISM." He asked for the younger scholar's "reaction and suggestions."[46] Carnell replied that he had "received the first of the series of articles which your [*sic*] are writing for that magazine on the truncated world-view of the fundamentalists." He concluded that "it is hard to submit any criticisms inasmuch as I agree with your position to the letter."[47] Little did the professors know that *Uneasy Conscience* would sell more than one hundred thousand copies and mark Henry as the top young evangelical scholar of his day.

Carnell also commented on Henry's *Remaking the Modern Mind*, a response to J. H. Randall's *Making the Modern Mind*. Carnell shared that he had "poured over it with great interest" and was "talking it up at Gordon" with "[m]any copies sold."[48] He related information from his Harvard training on the book's status: "Dr. Ferre, prof. of theology (neo-orthodox, so-called) at Andover Newton, told the boys in his classes that it was a good piece of work." He tacked on that Ferre suggested that "[a]ll it lacked was a positive defence of the orthodox faith. He doesn't want much in one volume." Henry responded by noting that one of the Boston scholars, "Kuhn of Asbury," had given "it a fine review in their journal, and Ferre sent me a nice note on it."[49]

At this time, Carnell felt the need to begin seeking out a more prestigious job. He knew of one that held his interest. Like many of his Christian peers, he had heard of just-started Fuller Theological Seminary and was aware that Henry was a member of the first faculty of the school. He yearned to join the action. Carnell knew Ockenga from his attendance at the church during his time in Boston. In December 1947, he noted to Henry that while he had joined his father's church in Lansing, Michigan, he would "fellowship with the congregation (Congregational) of Dr. Harold John Ockenga. I like his stentorian Reformed preaching."[50]

Carnell noted an attraction to the church due to the robust intellect displayed in Ockenga's sermons: "He gives a theological discourse in his fourty [*sic*] minute sermon and the people (1500–2000 strong) love it. It, to my mind, is a testimony to what really solid preaching can do. The church supports 61 missionaries." The pastor's "really solid preaching" drew the Carnells to Brimstone Corner for weekly worship following Ed's resignation of his pastorate at Marblehead. The fact that Ockenga preached a "theological discourse" in his messages signaled to Carnell that he was a pastor worth following, as did the church's missionary commitment.

It was in this time that Carnell got to know Ockenga. When he heard of the beginning of Fuller Theological Seminary, he wrote to Ockenga and registered a bold and persuasive appeal for consideration as a faculty member at the exciting new venture. First, he noted his unanimity of spirit with his preacher: "I have discovered that our world-views coincide almost jot for jot and tittle for tittle. You combine a happy appreciation of Reformation Christianity with a love for the Fundamentalists of our present day, an attitude which, I believe, by uniting a tear in the heart with the law of contradiction in our logic, will, in the long run, win." The point was plain enough: "I would love to work under you, Harold, to help shape and execute many of the ideals I know you nurture."[51]

Carnell did not lack for plans for himself and future colleagues. He referenced his long correspondence with Henry and noted a kinship with him: "For a period of years, Professor Henry and myself have fellowshipped together as we discussed things theological. . . . At that time we learned that, by collaboration, we could turn out many lectures, and, perhaps, volumes." The prospect of partnership had blossomed: "If I could take over the division that Dr. Henry is to lop off in time, that would solve the problem perfectly. Henry is now teaching both systematic theology and philosophy of religion. When he decides which field he would prefer, I would love to work over the other." This could mean, in time, "the publication of a series of contemporary volumes of great worth."[52]

Carnell went on in the letter to list his extensive and impressive credentials for a Fuller teaching post. This rather direct appeal to Ockenga reveals the closeness of theological vision shared by several of the leading neo-evangelicals. It also shows the connection between Henry and Carnell during their period of study in Boston.

The two not only enjoyed fellowship but desired on some level to "turn out many lectures" and "volumes." The accidental network of the Cambridge evangelicals carried great hopes for the rehabilitation of evangelical thought, at least in the minds of the students.

Before Carnell could launch into the scholarly stratosphere, he needed to finish his two degrees. In December 1947, he wrote to Henry that "[y]ou will be glad to know that the committee on my Th.D. at Harvard has been poring over my dissertation for almost two weeks now, and I should be, alas!, a doctor by the end of January. It took ten and one-half years, but it has been good discipline."[53] As he neared the close of his two doctorates, Carnell reflected on the difficulty and the significance of the task he and Henry had undertaken. In March 1948, he told his friend that he had "a mountain of term papers to face by the middle of April, plus my generals and German." His next statement speaks volumes for the feat he wished to pull off: "It is a grind and I am very tired, physically and mentally, but I look upon this discipline as preparatory for the rigor of dialectic to come when those opportunities are ours to snatch the leadership of evangelical scholarship in this generation."[54] Carnell possessed great hopes for the future of "evangelical scholarship" as it carried out "dialectic" with those that did not practice it.

Such an undertaking had not come without challenge for the German Reformer, and it would not for the Cambridge evangelical, either. Carnell wrote in March 1948 to Henry to share some comments from Brightman on an early draft of his dissertation. It was "brilliant," Brightman said.[55] He had "compared it to Bowne's first work as a student," extremely high praise for Carnell. Brightman went on to argue, though, that Carnell "define[d] Christian far too rigidly and narrowly for him, excluding modernists etc." He also apparently said that Carnell's "defense of sovereignty cancels out my rationalism." Carnell pointed out that this was "[a] real problem."

This kind of experience convinced the young theologian that he needed even more training in order to prepare himself adequately for theological disputation. He urged Henry to "go abroad, otherwise we shall be consigned to mediocrity."[56] Even in the midst of two high-level degrees, Carnell still felt his inadequacy for the task. Studying under many of the world's brightest theological minds, he considered himself "a big amateur" and knew that he would need all the credibility he could muster to begin to gain a hearing for his views. Still, Brightman clearly considered him a uniquely gifted pupil.

Evangelical scholars affirmed this gifting when they voted Carnell's *An Introduction to Christian Apologetics* the top apologetic book of 1947. A cable announced the award in a font that mirrored Carnell's outsized ambitions: "PROFESSOR EDWARD JOHN CARNELL IS WINNER OF THE $5,000.00 EERDMANS EVANGELICAL BOOK AWARD."[57] Henry had written the introduction to the volume and had suggested some weaknesses, which touched Carnell off a bit: "Whether your criticisms are too pointed and will injure the sale of the book or not, Mr. Eerdmans will have to decide. I would rather not take part in the question for personal reasons."[58] For his part, Henry encouraged Carnell to look at the abundantly bright side. Publishing the introductory volume was "a master stroke, and following it with a volume on Brunner will put the evangelicals in debt to you, with few equals."[59]

Henry was wrong about his not getting anything done, but right about Carnell's capacity for writing. Carnell's work at Harvard and Boston University had in general gone very well. In 1948, he graduated with his ThD from Harvard University.[60] In 1949, he graduated with a PhD from Boston University.[61] He had pulled off the unthinkable: two doctorates, completed simultaneously, from top-tier universities. His impressive example could not help but speak to a fresh intellectual interest among evangelicals.

Carnell would eventually publish both of his dissertations with Eerdmans. In 1950, Eerdmans debuted *The Theology of Reinhold Niebuhr*; in 1956, *The Burden of Søren Kierkegaard*.[62] Carnell was clearly part of a new generation of evangelical leaders. These leaders occupied diverse posts in distinct places in the evangelical and fundamentalist network. One key location was Boston. Even though Carnell and Henry did not have a great deal of time together in the city during their program, they nonetheless forged a bond in the Hub that foreshadowed future collaboration.

Carnell and Henry were not the only evangelical scholars of promise in the city, however. The greatest evangelical New Testament scholar of the next several decades was also plowing away. George Eldon Ladd was from humble, troubled origins but emerged in the course of his studies at Harvard Divinity School as one of the brightest of the pack. He had come to Harvard in 1944 after two years at Boston University in the doctoral program in classics. His time at Harvard was formative, as John D'Elia has observed: "The challenge—and intellectual freedom—of Harvard deeply influenced the rest of Ladd's life and career as a scholar, giving him a new framework through which he could support his evangelical faith."[63] The specifically "new critical manner in which Ladd learned to *hold his belief*" had perhaps an even greater influence on him than the content of his courses.[64] By 1949, Ladd had shown himself a student of great promise.

Ockenga initiated correspondence with Ladd in 1949 to recruit him to the faculty of Fuller Theological Seminary. Ladd responded with a lengthy statement of his research interests and teaching philosophy.[65] Though Ladd maintained a stoutly "supernaturalist" framework and traditional evangelical doctrinal commitments, his desired program of scholarship contrasted, in his mind, with that of his forebears:

> *Special interests.* . . . I have been brought up a premillennialist on the Scofield Bible and W.E.B. [theologian William E. Blackstone]; but I have long been dissatisfied with the uncritical and unscholarly character of most of the premillennarian literature. Therefore, I chose for two of my elective degree examinations the fields of "New Testament Eschatology" and "Two Jewish Apocalypses: Enoch and IV Ezra". Desiring to pursue the same interest in other areas, I

selected for my thesis subject "Chiliasm in the First Three Christian Centuries". As the subject opened up, it seemed wise to limit the theme more narrowly, and the final subject was "The Eschatology of the Didache". These studies have constituted the beginning of what is to be a life-long interest. There does not exist a scholarly history of the Kingdom of God concept in English from the premillennarian point of view; nor does there exist an adequate treatment of the Kingdom of God in the Gospels from this same view-point. This study is my present other interest, and I am now compiling bibliography and working through the periodical literature and shall produce as I have time and opportunity. I feel very keenly the need for a scholarly premillennial literature, and it is in this field that I hope to make my chief contribution.[66]

Ladd showed no hesitancy to criticize the fundamentalist tradition. He clearly intended to redress the shortcomings of past scholars by his own work. Yet Ladd's dismissal of much Christian scholarship that had preceded him had not disposed him to leave the guild but to work within it to strengthen its faith and practice. Here was the neo-evangelical scholarly impulse filtered through the lens of biblical studies: to build a better method and vindicate the faith in the presence of its detractors.

Just like Carnell, Ladd wished to aid Christians in the work of apologetics, the defense of the faith in a culture that had shifted away from it. This is clear in his stated "teaching philosophy":

Teaching philosophy. In the broader field of New Testament studies, my primary interest is in historical criticism. A definite philosophy dominates my teaching. Students should first of all be taught the basic content of the New Testament. They should be instructed in the best tools for study and the proper techniques for exegeting the Word. There is in addition a third most important principle: students should be taught to think through in a critical fashion the great questions of New Testament history. It has been my experience that critical studies have strengthened my confidence in the supernaturalistic interpretation of the origins of historical Christianity. It is my conviction that when a truly inductive method is employed in the study of the New Testament narratives, the student will discover that the traditional supernaturalistic interpretation best accounts for the data. When one studies critically the New Testament records and evaluates the several historical solutions which criticism has produced, one will find, I believe, *if his mind is open to it*, that the supernaturalistic interpretation best explains the facts. This is a great historical apologetic. I believe in the verbal inspiration of the Scriptures. I recognize also that the Bible is an historical record. Christianity is essentially an historical religion. When the student has been taught to think through the critical evaluations of this historical process, he will realize that his Faith upon [*sic*] historically sound foundations. This is not a method I have been taught; I have worked it out in my graduate studies. I have been testing it in my teaching at Gordon Divinity School and have found it warmly received by the students. This scientific method in New Testament studies will reinforce philosophical and theological approach, and will impart to students an uninhibited confidence in the integrity of our Faith.[67]

This was a carefully constructed model of Christian teaching. It did not shy away from the essential claim of orthodox Christianity, that it was a historical faith grounded in actual events and miraculous acts. Yet the faith and its leading proponents were not to shy away from the questions posed to it by "historical criticism," the discipline which pursued an authoritative account of "New Testament history." Exegetes did not need to leave scholarly tools by the side in making the case for the veracity of evangelical faith. Rather, evangelical academicians should pick these tools up, fasten them to their belt, and employ them.

In reconstructing the history of the Christian movement as attested in the Bible, one would inevitably find, according to Ladd, that "the supernaturalistic interpretation" best accounted for the data. That is, the God of the Bible orchestrated the events recorded in the twenty-seven books of the New Testament. In Ladd's view, fair though critically sensitive study led the open-minded student to this conclusion. Much had been made in Ladd's day of the supernatural nature of the faith; Ladd intended to uphold this idea even as he wished to show that the faith was profoundly historical. This was a bold program dedicated not merely to enhanced evangelical scholarship in its own right but also to the strengthening of Christian apologetics. This tested method would yield "an uninhibited confidence in the integrity of our faith."[68]

Ladd's desire to buttress the church's faith fit fluidly with Ockenga's broader interests at Fuller. In offering Ladd the position of Associate Professor of New Testament on April 10, 1950, to begin teaching on September 1, 1950, Ockenga expressed this aim: "Our desire is that our men will produce books in their own fields. There is an appalling lack of apologetic literature defending the Christian faith in our day, and we want our faculty to work as a unit in bringing this up-to-date."[69]

When Ladd responded to Ockenga's invitation, he spelled out further his aspirations for meeting this great need. His response from July 1950 is yet another rare and richly valuable window into the thinking behind the intellectual project attempted by the neo-evangelicals. Ladd shared a desire to master foreign literature in his discipline:

> An adequate evangelical scholarship, if it is to make a lasting impact, must control this German literature. It must be up to date and deal with these anti-evangelical positions at their source. My particular interest is eschatology, particularly that of the Gospels, and the Kingdom of God. A few of the important German books have been translated: Albert Schweitzer's *Von Reimarus zu Wrede*, Rudolf Otto's *Reich Gotes und Menschensohn*; but most of them are still in German: Arthur Titius *Jesus Lehre vom reiche Gottes* (1895), H. E. Weber, *Eschatologie und Mystik im N.T.*, H. D. Wendland, *Die Eschatologie des Reiches Gottes bei Jesus*, (1931), W. G. Hummel *Verheissung und Erfullung* (1945), G. Gloege *reich Gottes und Kirche in N.T.* (1929),

W. Michaelis Taufer, *Jesus, Urgemeinde, Die Predigt vom Reiche Gottes vor und nach Pfingsten* (1928), and many others. If one is to control and interpret this extensive literature with authority and take his stand in the midst of the intellectual movements of the day, he must master this material.[70]

Ladd clearly desired to push beyond his own religious sector in engaging the New Testament at a scholarly level. His training at Harvard had equipped him with the tools he needed to interact with scholars of New Testament from every tradition and viewpoint. It is perhaps his confidence that is most striking in this personal plan. Ladd believed that he could and should master this literature and answer it. He was not content merely to converse with evangelical scholars, important as that was. He wished for evangelical scholarship to dialogue with those who would not immediately receive its conclusions.

Ladd's later texts like *The Gospel of the Kingdom: Scriptural Studies in the Kingdom of God* (1959) and *Jesus and the Kingdom* (1964), reveal that he made good on his desire to produce "an adequate study of the Kingdom of God."[71] In order to produce these and other works and acquire a widely respected standing in the broader field of biblical studies, Ladd sought to acquire "a complete mastery of German" through several lengthy stays in that country. He charted an ambitious course in his writing, but more, he paid the cost necessary to win entrance to the elite guild.

These memorable words from one of the greatest New Testament scholars of the twentieth century speak volumes about the unusual aspirations of the Cambridge evangelicals. They believed that they were, like Billy Sunday, redeemed by divine grace. They too enjoyed evangelical fellowship and ministered in the context of the church. But unlike Sunday, they harbored unusual academic ambitions. They wanted to know, teach, and promote theology to a movement that was, one could say, as intellectually unprepared as a jackrabbit at a Harvard doctoral colloquium.

CHAPTER 4

GRAND STRATEGY BY THE BEACH

Ockenga and the Cultivation of the Cambridge Evangelicals

H arold John Ockenga did not have to work hard to discover the young prince of the resurgent evangelical movement. Edward John Carnell was right under his nose. Carnell was uniquely suited to the intellectual resurgence Ockenga came to desire. He was never going to be a globe-trotting evangelist like Graham, smooth as silk and firm in his handshake. With his tightly coiled temperament and slight frame, Carnell was made for a different world, the scholarly realm. In truth, he was as ideally suited to the academic classroom as Graham was to the football stadiums of his revival circuit. Carnell read and wrote in great volume. He processed quickly. But he was not dry and dusty. His prose crackled with electricity. At times, Carnell's boldness would get him into hot water, as when he criticized fundamentalism in the late 1950s for its small-mindedness. Early on, in the 1940s, it made him an ideal partner for the burgeoning neo-evangelical project.

Though Carnell was the brightest of the pack, he was just one of the Cambridge evangelicals, the group of brilliant young evangelical students at Harvard (and Boston University).[1] Ockenga would soon develop close contacts with this group. By the mid-1940s, Ockenga was one of a handful of well-known evangelicals, the president of the National Association of Evangelicals, a popular parachurch group he helped found that drew dozens of evangelical denominations together. By the mid-1940s alone, he had published seven books.[2] Park Street Church flourished, drawing more than two thousand members in the 1940s.[3] The congregation supported a horde of missionaries, another important ecclesial benchmark—110 by 1951.[4]

From his prominent position, Ockenga forged bonds and curated a common vision for a recalibrated Christian intellect through formal and informal means. In what follows, we look closely at Ockenga's work to build a new evangelical intellectualism through two lenses: first, his staging of a series of scholarly gatherings he called the Plymouth Scholars' Conferences, and second, his cultivation of relationships with the group known here as the Cambridge evangelicals.

In the middle years of the 1940s, Ockenga took a bold step toward the broader project of invigorating evangelical scholarship. He launched the Plymouth Scholars' Conferences, small gatherings that were held in 1944, 1945, and 1947 in various locales in New England.[5] Over the span of these events, he invited Ladd, Carnell, Henry, Tenney, Crum, and Lewis to attend. Each of these doctoral students came and gave papers for an eminent group of Christian theologians. Ockenga remembered this in his foreword to Harold Lindsell's *Battle for the Bible*: "[D]uring the summers of 1944 in 1945 I convened a group of theologians at Manomet Point, Massachusetts, to discuss the need for the writing of a new evangelical literature, based upon evangelical principles and, in particular, upon an inerrant Scripture." At this point, Ockenga suggested, "the evangelical movement had begun to grow" but "had to depend upon literature of a previous generation. Those two conferences brought evangelical scholars into contact with each other."[6]

The first meeting took place from August 25–30, 1944, at the elegant Mayflower Hotel in Manomet, Massachusetts. Ten scholars attended the event, listed in the official report as follows: Dr. Harold John Ockenga, Mr. John Bolten, Bishop Leslie Marston, Dr. William E. Powers, Mr. Culbert Rutenber, Dr. Cornelius Van Til, Dr. Clarence Bouma, Dr. H. C. Thiessen, Mr. Stacey Woods, and Mr. Terrelle B. Crum.[7] The report thanked Ockenga and Bolten "for their spiritual vision in planning such a gathering and for their kindness and generosity in providing such a delightful setting for the discussions at the Mayflower Hotel."[8] The document then listed several aims that future meetings of evangelical scholars could accomplish:

> *First*, a much needed *informal fellowship* would be provided for evangelical scholars, stimulating personal friendships, fresh insights into the truth of God and a more effectual prayer for each other's particular ministry.
>
> *Second*, a *clearer understanding and a practical definition of our common faith* would be achieved, thereby helping us to interpret the differences between our evangelical communions rather than in a divisive spirit.
>
> *Third*, as a normal outgrowth of this larger fellowship and understanding, the *production of scholarly literary works* would be stimulated, thus meeting the desperate need of the evangelical churches for reliable and readable statements of our common faith in itself and also as over against today's prevailing liberalism and unbelief.[9]

Ockenga intended for the gathering to produce unity rather than division. He believed that a unified group of thinkers could encourage "the production of scholarly literary works," meeting the great need of the day both for strong in-house teaching and for refutation of "liberalism and unbelief." As other documents cited in this study have displayed, the neo-evangelical academic impulse was twofold—to build evangelical faith and address secular thinking.

The first Plymouth gathering had a clear and unmistakable aim: to help believers recognize that "Christianity is intellectually defensible."

Each generation, the pastor believed, needed "to chart a new apologetic" that would demonstrate this claim and meet contemporary challenges to the faith. In a moderated tone, Ockenga suggested that many "able evangelists, pastors and teachers" existed to undertake "Kingdom work." The central problem of the day was not a lack of vigorous preaching and zealous evangelism. Pastors like Ockenga believed that the "declaration of the Gospel" was the cornerstone of their work. They required help, however, from Christian scholars. "Apologetic defense" had to be offered by "the Christian professor, not the evangelist or pastor."

The second conference, held in 1945, was on "Training Ministers For The Post-War World," as Ockenga reported to Henry.[10] Subtopics were "Exegesis, Biblical Theology, Systematics, Apologetics, The Christian Weltanschauung, and Practical Theology, with an emphasis upon Biblical Theology rather than Historical Theology." The event, held from August 13–17, 1945, at the Mayflower Hotel, drew an impressively diverse array of Christian theologians: Ockenga (the chairman), Cornelius Van Til, Clarence Bouma of Calvin Theological Seminary, William Emmett Powers of Eastern Baptist Theological Seminary, Henry C. Thiessen of Wheaton College, Stacey Woods of InterVarsity Christian fellowship, Terrelle Crum of the Providence Bible Institute, T. Leonard Lewis, president of Gordon College, Allan Macrae of Faith Theological Seminary, Merrill Tenney, P. B. Fitzwater of Moody Bible Institute, Henry, Everett Harrison of Dallas Theological Seminary, and John Bolten (the host).[11] In addition to Tenney's paper, Fitzwater spoke on systematic theology, Bouma on "Theocentric ethics," and Van Til on "The Christian Weltanschauung."

One of the event's core motivations was the "stimulation" of scholarly evangelical literature. The official report of the conference registered the difficulties working against such an end, citing the demands of "necessary research, over-loaded schedules, and the limits of human strength."[12] Nevertheless, the participants promised to one another as scholarly blood-brothers that they would produce the literature in question. For example, Van Til looked forward to the publication of a volume titled *The New Modernism* that would address the "dialectical theologians."[13]

The attendees sketched grand plans around the table. The minutes registered their desire to establish "an annual lectureship" which would facilitate relief from "teaching duties" for a semester and the publication of "a book manuscript."[14] They also wanted to produce "a series of Old and New Testament commentaries, by cooperative effort, over a period of years."[15] Ideally, this series would represent "truly high and respected scholarship" and would be printed by one of "the most reputable publishers," outfits like "Macmillan, Scribners and Harper Brothers."[16] Furthermore, the group wished to establish "a graduate summer school" that would allow "for advanced work on a high level."[17] Finally, the scholars wished to produce a new version of the "International Standard Bible Encyclopedia" characterized by "conservative scholarship."[18] Along with several other short-term goals, these initiatives marked the prospective outcome of the Plymouth gathering.

The final conference met in the summer of 1947. In his invitation letters, Ockenga continued to sound the horn for a "new apologetic literature" aimed at the "college and university students of our day."[19] He outlined the Plymouth gathering's main topic, "Inspiration and Revelation," in a letter to Crum and suggested his hope that "every man will at least contribute an article to some theological journal, and secondly, that he might be stimulated in the writing of a book."[20] In his communication to Henry, Ockenga noted that he "was not entirely satisfied with the last two conferences for the advancement of evangelical scholarship. I do believe that they could be much more useful and meaningful than they have been."[21]

Henry wrote back to accept the invitation and let Ockenga know of the prospect of an evangelical translation of the Bible: "Now a further note, in utmost confidence, which comes as a result of recent conference with VanKampen Press here in Chicago. As you know, most readers of the New Testament are evangelicals; many of the liberals get around to the Bible only for critical purposes." Despite this fact, "liberals" produced the new translations, causing all kinds of problems for genuinely evangelical organizations. Henry proposed a new plan, showing his strategic impulse: "Why in the world do we not turn out an evangelical translation? We have Mantey at Northern, Tenney at Wheaton, Thiessen at Los Angeles, Ladd at Gordon, Buswell at National Bible Institute, etc.—all of them competent Greek scholars. The big lack would be funds—but would be a better stroke than something of this sort?"[22]

Henry had clearly taken the thrust of the conferences to heart. He wished to tap the growing network of evangelical academicians— including fellow Boston scholars Tenney and Ladd—to produce a new translation sensitive to evangelical concerns. Henry's communication with Ockenga suggests that evangelical scholars had formed nascent bonds and were in the process of establishing an informal identity.[23]

Ockenga brought a number of other scholars into the fold, though some had to decline. Joseph P. Free of the Wheaton department of Anthropology and Archaeology wrote on May 17, 1947, to decline. He noted before closing that "[f]or several years I have felt the need of just the type of thing you are doing, and have wished that encouragement might be given to fundamentalist scholars to produce the literature that we need."[24] The Boston pastor had clearly identified a need that many perceived but that few addressed, at least on a public level, to say nothing of an organizational one.

The scholar who expressed the most excitement over Ockenga's vision was Carnell. As previously noted, Carnell and Ockenga had become acquainted during the former's time in Boston, and Carnell worshipped at Park Street Church. Ockenga saw fit to invite the brilliant young thinker to the third conference, an action that summoned forth Carnell's lively prose and passionate convictions on the matter of the Christian mind:

Yours of the 29th was received in good order. I accept with alacrity your kind offer to join with other men in the country for discussion of the Faith with the end to stimulate the production of Christian apologetic literature. It would be superfluous for me to tell you how grateful to you I am for this opportunity to mingle with the leaders of our cause. I am certain it is of grace and not of merit that I join with these outstanding pioneers in the various departments of the theological encyclopedia. Whatever small contribution I may be able to make will certainly be done cheerfully, for I am all too aware of the anemic state of the Christian organism in the world today.[25]

Carnell then doubled down: "I am champing at the bit, as it were, to see this conference be a tremendous success," because it offered a "first step" toward a renewal of evangelical thought.

Carnell's prose soared yet higher. "I am possessed with a whole-soul conviction," he wrote, that the way to restore "the glory of the church of Jesus Christ is a thorough shakedown of our educational program, from the grade school to the graduate divisions of our universities." There was no other way to make the jump in Carnell's eyes. "We must have scholars to put our movement into print, both negatively to compete with Rome, neo-orthodoxy, and communism, and affirmatively to place before the intelligentsia a *Weltanschauung* which will make peace with the law of contradiction horizontally and which will vertically fit the facts of history."[26]

This was a bold statement revealing a strong degree of academic confidence bred of elite training. The Cambridge evangelicals emphasized the explanatory power of the Christian *Weltanschauung*, as Carnell called it, or what Henry called the "Christian world-and-life view."[27] Popularized at the turn of the century by figures like Abraham Kuyper, Prime Minister of the Netherlands from 1901 to 1905, Christian worldview thinking emphasized the "sphere sovereignty" of Jesus Christ and the cohesiveness of biblical thought. Kuyper's famous dictum put it, "There is not one square of creation over which Jesus Christ does not cry 'Mine!'"[28] As the century wore on, the Reformed tradition expounded upon this principle, suggesting that biblical truth applied to all of life and thought and that Christianity wielded explanatory power in every realm due to its coherence in the Lord and Master of the cosmos, Jesus Christ. This worldview approach catalyzed many of the Cambridge evangelicals and their scholarly peers. The tradition in question allowed the young thinkers to locate themselves within a historic tradition grounded in a cohesive intellectual framework.

In recent days, the neo-evangelicals have received criticism for their over-confidence in worldview thinking. Molly Worthen has said of the neo-evangelicals that their project, building momentum in the decade in question, eventually yielded a "crude but compelling public theology" that nonetheless was not "totally coherent."[29] There is no doubt some truth here; the bark of the neo-evangelicals could outpace their scholarly bite. But this characterization undersells the nature of the neo-evangelical enterprise. They genuinely thought that they could reinvigorate the "Christian organism," as Carnell memorably put it, and they made some significant progress in developing public theology through both institutions and books, as later chapters will show.

The theme of Plymouth Conference of 1947 was "Inspiration and Revelation."[30] The event ran from June 23 to 27, 1947, and was held at the New Ocean House in Magnolia, Massachusetts. A number of prior attendees came: Henry, Harrison, Crum, Ockenga, Woods, and Bolten, in addition to Carnell of Gordon, Ned Stonehouse of Westminster Theological Seminary, Theodore Graebner of Concordia Seminary, Harry Jellema of the University of Indiana, Arnold Schultz of Northern Baptist Theological Seminary, and R. Laird Harris of Faith Theological Seminary.[31] The gathering featured papers such as Carnell's "Progressive Revelation as a Solution to the Alleged Moral Difficulties and Contradictions to the Doctrine of Scriptural Infallibility." In general, discussion ranged over the following concerns:

1. Recent use of revelation and inspiration as grounded in nineteenth century evolutionary critical thought.
2. Progressive revelation as opposed to evolutionary development of religious consciousness.
3. Progressive revelation as the solution to the alleged moral difficulties and contradictions.
4. Historical survey of the theories of inspiration.
5. Difficulties in verbal inspiration.
6. Does archaeological investigation conserve the Christian view of revelation and inspiration? And how?
7. Textual criticism and divine inspiration.
8. Alleged difficult contradictions of Scriptural infallibility.
9. Is it possible to maintain Biblical revelation and inspiration without accepting Biblical infallibility?[32]

The impact of these gatherings was "enormous" in the judgment of one scholar.[33] The scholars enjoyed conversation and theologically driven dialogue in a constructive, friendly atmosphere. Ockenga ran a tight ship, creating a charged atmosphere over several days. The conferences allowed for both formal and informal discussion. Ockenga's plans for previous conferences noted the need for both, particularly in the elegant location in which the gatherings occurred: "We usually spend part of the morning on the presentation of a subject and then we adjourn to the beach where discussions take place during most of the day if the weather is acceptable."[34] One can imagine that the scholars did not mind this sort of arrangement, with its provision both for theological exchange and ultraviolet exposure.

The Plymouth conferences did not eventuate directly in a series of texts or an ongoing lectureship. Aside from a few press releases, we can trace few public products of the gatherings themselves. Yet the conferences played a crucial role in the project to rehabilitate and strengthen the evangelical mind. The Plymouth gatherings showed the attendees that others shared their burdens and goals. Ockenga intended for Plymouth to showcase, furthermore, how the theological disciplines could pollinate one another. Great gains would come from theologians speaking with philosophers, exegetes interacting with apologists, ministry workers conversing with church historians.

Because of Ockenga, a collective drive to renew the mind of conservative American Protestantism began to coalesce in the scholars' conferences. The initial setting of Plymouth was a fitting choice, if a rather obvious one. The Pilgrims had made their own fresh start on its shores in 1620. Ockenga's conferences sought a new beginning for a movement stripped of its academic credentials. Much had been accomplished to this point, but the neo-evangelical intellectual vision was still forming. The real work had only just begun.

Ockenga was up to the task. Beyond Plymouth, he popped up repeatedly in the correspondence and activity of the Cambridge evangelicals. Henry preached in the "historic house" of Park Street and in 1946 asked Ockenga to write the foreword to *The Uneasy Conscience of Modern Fundamentalism*.[35] In the foreword, Ockenga noted that "Dr. Henry has put his finger on what is troubling us."[36] This commendation, from a Reformed pastor who was the leading neo-evangelical figure of the time, the man who had invented the term "neo-evangelicalism," meant a great deal to the book and its success. Bearing the imprimatur of such a trusted figure, *Uneasy Conscience* sold well over one hundred thousand copies. Ockenga not only interacted with the scholars; he helped mint them.

E. J. Carnell found Ockenga's preaching especially strong. During much of his time in Boston, he worshipped at Park Street; he noted to Henry that he loved Ockenga's "stentorian reformed preaching."[37] Other members of the informal group of the Cambridge evangelicals responded similarly. Gleason Archer Jr. sought out employment under Ockenga at Park Street during the mid-1940s. Ockenga trained him for ministry, employed him as minister to college students, and hired him at Fuller.

Harold Lindsell was another young scholar at Harvard (MA) who flocked to Ockenga. The man who would later singlehandedly divide evangelicalism over the issue of inerrancy connected with Ockenga in the 1940s in his student days before writing the first biography of the pastor, *Park Street Prophet*, in 1951. Years later, Lindsell's remarks show reverence for Ockenga: "Many people regarded him with a sense of awe, for he seemed to reign from Olympian heights.... The students in the first class at Fuller Theological Seminary passed along an apocryphal story about how they rose at six in the morning, turned to the East where Harold lived as in-absentia president of the institution, and bowed down three times."[38] From the laudatory tones of *Park Street Prophet*, Lindsell's biography of Ockenga, it was clear that he himself was in his thrall as a young academician.

Kenneth Kantzer was similarly impressed by the Boston preacher. He encountered Ockenga during his work as a graduate student worker at Harvard. Following Ockenga's final retirement, Kantzer remembered that "Dr. Ockenga always checked more books out of the library than any other area pastor—or even faculty member or student (except one)."[39]

Ockenga made use of his burgeoning connections to the Cambridge evangelicals. In time, Henry, Lindsell, Ladd, Archer, Carnell, Jewett, and Barker all would assume posts in Pasadena. Ockenga also had connections to Roger Nicole and Burton Goddard, faculty members at Gordon Divinity School, due to his role as a board member, a position he held from 1936 to 1969, when he became president of the school.[40]

All this fraternizing led to the formation of friendships that lasted for many decades. Henry later noted the profitable nature of his connection with his fellow evangelicals while in Boston. "The Boston locale," he noted in his autobiography, "shaped early associations with other Gordon divinity school men like George Eldon Ladd and Roger Nicole."[41] Because of his friendship with Nicole, Henry planned to write with the French theologian in his Fuller years and advocated that Nicole be hired at Fuller in part for this reason: "My own conviction is that [Roger] Nicole can be successfully encouraged in production, and that he and I could, at close range, jointly venture the task of a complete systematic theology."[42] No such venture happened, and Nicole never proved able to complete his own systematic theology, but the two shared a kinship and worked together in ventures like the Evangelical Theological Society.

A remarkable convergence of young evangelical talent took place in 1940s Boston, a development that Ockenga eventually recognized and shepherded. Years afterward, John A. Huffman Sr., Ockenga's co-pastor in the period in question, reflected on these heady days.[43] Huffman studied at Boston University during this period.

He remembered one professor at the university named David D. Vaughn who "would rant and rail at the evangelicals and Christians and he would sometimes quote "'there is power, power, wonder-working power in the blood of the lamb' and he would go 'baaa baaa baaa'—he hissed this." Despite this mockery, Huffman avowed that "deep in [Vaughn's] heart, he would respect a person who believed what he at one time believed and lost. And I had many experiences with teachers like that."[44]

While he served under Ockenga, Huffman discovered that the most promising students at Harvard "were not Unitarians, they were our evangelical boys." In his interview, Huffman struggled to remember names but referenced "Harold Kuhn one of them, Kenneth Kantzer another." These and a group of others he could not directly name "went to Harvard, and they made a good record at Harvard, they were serious, and Harvard was low on scholarship, and for a period of ten years there the best students at Harvard, carrying the best records were evangelical boys that didn't change their beliefs one bit."[45]

These are valuable reminisces. Huffman was on the ground in the period in question, and he repeatedly identified a common evangelical mentality among the pack of bright young evangelicals in Boston. He also gave pride of place in his recollections to the central role of Harold Ockenga. Through the pastor's efforts, and the developing friendships between more than a dozen bright young evangelical scholars, momentum was building for a greater project, one that would reach far beyond the historic city of Boston and the windswept beaches of Plymouth.

CHAPTER 5

Acts of Intellectual Daring

Ockenga and Henry on the Evangelical Mind

In a friendly, calm tone, Charles Fuller called his radio listeners, some twenty-million strong, to the cross: "Friend of mine, seated by the radio listening to this broadcast, outside of Christ—God is not willing that you should perish, but that you should come to repentance."[1] This simple, even humble, presentation characterized the midcentury phenomenon known as the *Old Fashioned Revival Hour.* Fuller's program was not only the most popular evangelical radio show in the 1940s; it was the most popular radio show of any kind in this era. During its run on the ABC network, the program was heard on more than 650 stations. Many years after it aired, Fuller's son Daniel remembered that, on average, the show received more than four hundred pieces of mail reporting salvific "decisions" each week.[2] Fuller's mailing list exceeded three hundred thousand people, making him a one-man marketing firm for doctrinally conservative Christianity.[3]

Fuller may have kept a humble profile, but he was a powerful

figure. With a platform like his, he became one of the key statesmen of the post-fundamentalist period, helping to form the National
Association of Evangelicals in 1942 and keeping up continual correspondence with key leaders of the newly emerging "neo-evangelical"
project. Fuller occupied a privileged position even among the evangelical illuminati, however, for his radio show, and the wealth he accrued
from it and his father's lucrative orange-growing business enabled
him to do more than just meet on committees and daydream by the
beach. The radio personality was well-groomed, gifted in salesman-
ship, and filthy rich. If he set his mind to something, Charles Fuller
could almost singlehandedly bring it to life.

He had just such a notion in 1946. Fuller wanted to start a
Christian seminary that would vindicate the faith and reload the evangelical movement. Once a fighting fundamentalist, he had become an
enthusiastic proponent of the vision championed by Ockenga, Billy
Graham, and others of a united evangelical front over and against a
separatist fundamentalist fortress. Fuller was a gifted preacher, but
he was not personally interested in taking on scholarly work. He was,
however, keenly interested in starting a seminary. He needed one
essential component, however: a president and visionary who could
instantiate his own dream on an "evangelical Cal Tech."[4]

Harold John Ockenga was the figure best suited to the task.
Ockenga had both excellent academic credentials—academic work
at Princeton, Westminster, and the University of Pittsburgh—and
a fulsome academic vision. We witness the unfolding of this vision
in his 1947 Fuller convocation address, "Challenge to the Christian
Civilization of the West." Ockenga was not alone in hatching grand
plans in this time. In 1947, Carl F. H. Henry published his landmark
text, *The Uneasy Conscience of Modern Fundamentalism.*[5]

In Ockenga's writings and Henry's book, we observe a striking
confluence of strategy and ideas. Both evangelical leaders championed a full-scale educational program characterized by engagement
with nonevangelical thought and confidence in the ability of Christian

institutions to sustain such engagement. As we will see, Charles Fuller's seed money and broadcast enabled the shared outlook of Ockenga and Henry, neo-evangelism's two most important intellectual strategists, to take on institutional expression in 1947.

By the 1940s, Ockenga had already formed this vision. His work with the Boston School of the Bible and the Plymouth Scholars' Conferences demonstrates that he believed firmly in the need for a fresh intellectual defense of Christianity built on rigorous scholarship. Neither of the ventures satisfied his ambitions, however. He was restless and ready for a bigger challenge. When radio evangelist Charles Fuller contacted him in 1946 with a vision for a new educational institution, Ockenga made clear his desire for a divinity school. He noted that he and others had "been trying to build up a strong seminary here at Gordon College and are succeeding in part, but we lack the needed resources to make it the kind of school we would have it to be."[6] Despite this fact, Ockenga offered that "a wonderful beginning has been made."

As happened at various points in his life, the pastor's words foreshadowed a later development. The Fuller-Ockenga correspondence developed quickly into a courtship and then a contract. Fuller contacted a number of Christian leaders, including Wilbur Smith of Moody Bible Institute and Lewis Sperry Chafer, president of Dallas Theological Seminary, but he found no one willing or able to take on the essential task before him: identifying a leader to serve as president of the "evangelical Cal Tech" he so desired.

Ockenga soon emerged as the figure best suited to this high-flown role. Daniel Fuller noted years later that his father and others regarded Ockenga as "a prime leader of evangelicals" because of his earning of a doctorate and his leadership of a historic Boston church.[7] As a Christian statesman himself, Charles Fuller relished the opportunity to draw a leader who had established himself as one of the most prominent evangelical voices in these essential spheres of activity. For his part, Ockenga thrilled to such a major undertaking. At an April 1947 meeting in the prestigious Union League Club of Chicago, Ockenga announced before a coterie of distinguished evangelical thinkers that he would serve as "president *in absentia*." Ockenga outlined his duties, as recounted by Fuller: "He would work to recruit the charter faculty and map out the curriculum."[8]

The preacher had already begun the work, in fact. He drew on his connections to several of the Cambridge evangelicals to begin seeding the school. On March 12, 1947, he suggested "[a]s Professor of Apologetics and Christian Ethics Dr. Carl Henry of Northern who has a Th.D. and will soon have his Ph.D. As Librarian Mr. Terrelle Crum of Providence Bible Institute who soon will have his Ph.D. from Harvard and who is an exceedingly able man."[9] Finally, "As Dean and Secretary of the Faculty Dr. Gleason Archer, who is equipped to teach in several fields." These gifted scholars shared a common theological orientation: "All these men are Calvinistic but are broad Calvinists. They would fit into such a school."[10]

Ockenga also advocated the hiring of Terrelle Crum and Merrill Tenney.[11] In addition, yet another Cambridge evangelical who had studied for a master's degree at Harvard, Harold Lindsell, came up: "I have had a long talk with Dr. Harold Lindsell yesterday in reference to our registration forms, the schedule of courses, the semesters, the limit of students, the degrees, etc."[12] Lindsell could serve in an administrative role even as he taught at the school.

Ockenga also brought Carnell to Fuller's attention: "I have suggested Professor Edward Carnell of Gordon College, who is taking his Doctor of Theology at Harvard this year and will [*sic*] his Doctor of Philosophy next year from Boston University and has a very keen mind and is a fine scholar."[13] Ockenga did not only recruit from the pool of mostly Harvard-trained men. He invited Wilbur Smith of Moody Bible Institute and Everett Harrison of Dallas Theological Seminary to form the first faculty of Fuller. It is clear, however, that he drew deeply from his well of connections to the Cambridge evangelicals to assemble the school's teachers.

In the end, these two, with Henry and Lindsell, constituted the initial professorial corps of the school.[14] In time, Archer, Ladd, Carnell, Paul King Jewett, and Glenn Barker would join these Boston-trained academicians. Ockenga had recruited extensively from the pool of bright young evangelical minds from his backyard. For these and other reasons, he believed that the seminary stood on solid ground as it opened in the fall of 1947 and that it might accomplish great things for the evangelical cause. He said to the school's namesake and benefactor: "I hope that as the days go by we will be able to blaze a trail of evangelical scholarship that will not close its eyes to such facts as these so as to make itself a butt on the part of educated secular men and on the other hand which will be able to defend the truth as it ought to be defended."[15] As Ockenga saw it, Fuller was not merely to offer an evangelical curriculum at a seminary level. Though it began small, with just four faculty, a president who lived three thousand miles away, and was funded by a busy radio evangelist responsible for a media empire, the school had a bold charter.[16]

Fuller saw itself as the first neo-evangelical academic institution. Ockenga brooked no disagreement in his conception of the school's identity. As he articulated for years after its founding, Fuller was not fundamentalist. Fundamentalism, he said portentously, had run aground. He charged that it had failed in a talk titled "Theological Education" given in the 1950s: "For decades fundamentalism has proved itself impotent to change the theological and ecclesiastical scene. Its lack of influence has relegated it to the peripheral and subsidiary movements of Protestantism." The matter was plain. Fundamentalism, as Ockenga construed it, was a losing ball club: "Wherever fundamentalism and modernism came into test in a theological struggle, fundamentalism lost every major battle in the historical field. It has demonstrated little power to crack the social situation challenging the church today."[17]

These were strong words. The hope for the next phase of evangelical life in America would not come, Ockenga made clear, from fundamentalist circles. Only neo-evangelicalism, imbued with a more positive doctrinal spirit, could advance the American Protestant cause. Ockenga and his peers had no less passion for evangelism than their fundamentalist counterparts, however. They did, however, wish to marry scholarship and evangelism. Evangelism alone would not prove enough for the task at hand, the recovery of America. Like the "tradition as extending back through Calvin to Augustine and the Apostle Paul," Ockenga and his peers wanted both to save souls and to save societies.

Ockenga gave vent to the *spirit* of intellectual neo-evangelicalism—and early Fuller—in Ockenga's convocation address at Fuller Theological Seminary in September 1947.[18] Fuller opened its doors on Monday, September 29, 1947, allowing its thirty-nine students to register that day. Faculty members had streamed in throughout the summer and much work remained to put the school in order. Initially, a good number of faculty and students took lodging in the just-purchased Cravens mansion that would house the school in its early days. Ockenga had designed the coursework in consultation with Henry and also Lindsell. The first students of the school took Greek and New Testament Introduction from Harrison, theology and philosophy of religion with Henry, apologetics with Wilbur Smith, and church history with Lindsell.

Word-of-mouth about the fledgling institution had yet to spread widely, but Fuller's recruiting efforts on *The Old-Fashioned Revival Hour* coupled with an announcement in the NAE's *United Evangelical Action* had drawn an already impressive crop of students from schools like Harvard, Dartmouth, and Berkeley. Bill Bright, later the founder of parachurch ministry Campus Crusade for Christ, was among them.[19]

When the fledgling seminary assembled for its first convocation on Wednesday, October 1, 1947, in the Pasadena Civic auditorium, the sense of a new beginning was palpable. Around twenty-five hundred people had come, a remarkable number for such a small institution.[20]

The weight of the moment was not lost on Ockenga, who exulted in such opportunities. Stepping to the microphone after the singing of several historic hymns, Ockenga delivered his message, titled "The Challenge to the Christian Culture of the West."[21] The crisp, hard-driving message offered something of a Western Civilization class in one hour. Its significance is great for the neo-evangelical project and the culture of intellectual engagement it helped create.

The copy of the address that has survived in the Ockenga papers includes a remarkable summary of the talk by Henry. First, Henry noted that "Dr. Ockenga used the word 'west' in two distinct connotations in this address."[22] The first usage referred to "its larger, historical, cultural and ethnic sense in which it refers to western civilization," and the second, "its lesser sense of referring to America's west as an incipient culture." Ockenga's talk did not suffer from intellectual immodesty; he attempted to challenge an entire culture in his address.

Henry pointed out the purposefully theological and philosophical nature of the message. Ockenga suggested that this era offered evangelicals "an unusual opportunity educationally" in which they could develop "the theological leaders of the future." The pastor, Henry noted, believed that seminaries like Fuller had a special and generally underappreciated role in producing such leaders: "Christian colleges and Bible Institutes are necessary to Christian education, but the key to the faith of the churches, and therefore to the moral fiber of the people, rests in the theological seminaries." This meant that "[t]he west must have a great theological seminary which will participate in the cultural development not only of America's west, but of western culture."

Ockenga began his message with Rome. Christianity had exerted a powerful effect on the Roman Empire, according to the preacher: "The dialectic of the Hebrew Christian tradition actually conquered the Roman civilization during the first three centuries. This power of heathendom crumbled under the impact of the Christian message."[23]

By the third century, Roman leaders, including the emperor (presumably Constantine), became "members of the church." This resulted in "the triumph of Christian principles." As such, "The foundations of the west were laid."[24]

In the Middle Ages, Ockenga suggested, "Art, music, literature, politics and economics were theocentric." However, at the same time, the Renaissance created a philosophical climate in which "[m]an became the measure of all things." The theocentric and anthropocentric tendencies clashed before the latter yielded "the modern secularistic spirit" marked by "scientific naturalism."[25] The pastor recounted his experience as a postwar member of the Commission of the United States War Department "investigating the conditions in Europe." He witnessed in biblical terms "the wake of the four horsemen who have ravaged Europe over a period of years." This terrible state traced back to philosophers of the "German enlightenment," including Kant and his "repudiation of God," Hegel's concept of "thesis, antithesis and synthesis," Darwin's "theory of evolution" which Marx used to produce "his theory of scientific naturalism and economic determinism," Nietzsche's "doctrine of force," and Spengler's "plea" for "the willingness to initiate a new culture." All this "intellectual preparation" and its "resultant destruction" was realized "in Hitler."[26]

This did not bode well for America in the mid-twentieth century, for "scientific naturalism" represented the "dominant intellectual current" of the day.[27] This, coupled with major decline in Germany before the war and in Ockenga's day in America, suggested a grave future for the west. The profligate conditions of wartime would result, the pastor warned, in "a new generation, half-German, half-American" or "half-German and half-Russian" or "half-German and half-British." Though Germany was "the home of the Reformation," a place "where reform and revival originated and spread throughout Europe," following the rise of "Higher Criticism" in the German schools, the Bible's authority diminished and led figures like Ritschl, Schleiermacher, and Harnack to apply "evolution to Christianity." This emptied out the

Christianity of the German people, leading to the rise of Marxism, which "caused the creation of Hitler and Nazism."[28]

Ockenga cited Hitler's *Mein Kampf* as arguing that "the economic materialism of Marx had nothing to resist it in Germany." It was Communism that formed "the inner conflict of western culture" in the postwar period. The ideology had created a long line of suffering marked by "hideous brutalities of Concentration Camps," "murdered war prisoners," "mass starvation," and more. In America, "promiscuity, delinquency," and "divorce" chewed away the country's ethical fabric. This had left America in a perilous position: "the moral effects of a Christian civilization no longer exist where the basic theories of the Christian civilization are gone."

Ockenga then turned his focus to fundamentalism. The movement, he argued, "failed to grasp" the "connection of our faith with the cultural question." He characterized the fundamentalist understanding of the world's social condition: "It is often thought that our preaching has nothing to do with the social conditions in the world. Fundamentalism has often shown a total disregard of questions of war, of lawlessness, of crime, of immorality, social theory, affirming that the purpose of the gospel in this age was merely to call people out for an other worldly existence." The neo-evangelicals and fundamentalists held similar theological convictions, but disagreed sharply in terms of the church's social program and cultural posture. Ockenga took pains to spell out the differences between the two movements.

Ockenga next considered the "Challenge to Christians in the West." He suggested that one could ground "the free man" and "the ethical man" only in "the principles of western culture."[29] Only a "theological institution" could reassert these long-cherished principles and produce an "apologetic literature" that would allow for the reconstruction of "the foundations of society." Here the Fuller president paused to note his work with the Plymouth conferences: "Long have I been interested in this and for this purpose I created what was called an Annual Conference for The Advancement of Evangelical

Scholarship, which has been meeting yearly in the east. Now in the providence of God it becomes possible to found a theological institution which will lay hold of and grapple with these problems as few are grappling with them today."[30]

Ockenga followed by stating his vision for the school in this period of neo-evangelical ascendancy: "Since in the minds of many people the ground work for the Christian view of God, the world, man and the kingdom has been destroyed by naturalism and liberalism, it will be the solemn and sacred duty of this faculty to attempt the reconstruction of this with scholarly pursuit."[31] In the discharging of this considerable duty, the school wished "to be ecclesiastically free" and to "cooperate with all evangelical denominations." The neo-evangelicals, led by Ockenga, intended to "repudiate the 'Come outist' movement which brands all denominations as apostate" and to "be positive in our emphasis," an emphasis grounded "on the broad doctrinal basis of a low Calvinism."

Fuller had made a promising start. But Ockenga had greater plans for the school. It was to be an academic powerhouse: "Our standard will require every faculty member to be an accepted and recognized scholar in his own field. Of these there will be ten heads of departments. We expect every student to be a graduate of an accepted college and to be screened to high spiritual and intellectual standards. We wish to take every advantage of intellectual training and background."[32] Ockenga had given Fuller a boldly intellectual charter.

"The Challenge to the Christian Culture of the West" is a crucial artifact of the neo-evangelical period, particularly for studies of the resurgent intellectualism of the postwar era. The text does not claim to speak for all of Ockenga's fellow believers, but it articulates better than most any other document the vision that inspired the pastor and his colleagues to attempt the bold move of founding a seminary. The message reveals that the scope of Ockenga's vision extended far beyond the traditional purpose and mandate of a seminary. Fuller existed to train pastors but also to trumpet the neo-evangelical conviction that Christianity provided not only the means of salvation for sinners but the only sure foundation for a civilized nation.

Ockenga was not alone in issuing such a call to his fellow evangelicals. Carl Henry was a strong partner in the work, one whose publishing carried his message all over the world. Henry's *The Uneasy Conscience of Modern Fundamentalism* sold more than one hundred thousand copies following its publishing in 1947.[33] The text bore a foreword from Ockenga, who suggested that "[t]he church needs a progressive Fundamentalism with a social message." The Bible applied not only to evangelism but to all of life: "A Christian world-and-life-view embracing world questions, societal needs, personal education ought to arise out of Matt. 28:18–21 as much as evangelism does. Culture depends on such a view, and Fundamentalism is prodigally dissipating the Christian culture accretion of centuries, a serious sin." Henry's short corrective, comprising just eighty-nine pages, offered a "healthy antidote" for this sorry situation, according to Ockenga.

Henry began his text with a stern indictment of fundamentalism. It lacked "social passion" and functioned as "the modern priest and Levite, by-passing suffering humanity." Henry, we might note, did not write *Uneasy Conscience* to immediately distance himself altogether from fundamentalism. Ockenga did, as his denunciation of "come-outism" suggested.[34] The neo-evangelicals had some disagreement on this point. Kenneth Kantzer, for example, skewered attacks on fundamentalists in an unpublished sermon, noting his doctrinal sympathy with their rock-ribbed belief in "the deity of Christ, the virgin birth, the bodily resurrection from the dead, the second coming of Christ, the atoning death of Christ, [and] the inerrancy of the Bible as the very written Word of God."[35] As time wore on, Henry, Kantzer, and others ceased to publicly identify themselves with the fundamentalist movement. This break was precipitated by the controversy that broke out in 1957 when fundamentalist leader Bob Jones Sr. opposed the decision of Billy Graham to seat nonevangelical ministers on his platform during his evangelistic campaigns.[36] After this crisis event and the print war that ensued, many of the neo-evangelicals distanced themselves from the fundamentalist label.

There was already serious tension between the two camps in the mid-1940s when Henry's book appeared. In chapter 6 of *Uneasy Conscience*, titled "The Struggle for a New World Mind," Henry argued that "[i]f historic Christianity is again to compete as a vital world ideology, evangelicalism must project a solution for the most pressing world problems."[37] One could locate the capital for such a solution in the gospel-shaped worldview: "The redemptive message has implications for all of life; a truncated life results from a truncated message." Where the church had failed, non-Christian authorities were glad to step in, according to Henry: "today secular education largely involves as open or subtle undermining of historic Christian theism."[38]

This precarious situation demanded "two great academic changes" of evangelicalism in Henry's estimation. "First, it must develop a competent literature in every field of study, on every level from the grade school through the university, which adequately presents each subject with its implications from the Christian as well as non-Christian points of view."[39] Beyond this, "[E]vangelicalism must not let the fact that the state has now become an agent of indoctrination obscure the evangelical obligation to press the Christian world-life view upon the masses. The church and the publishing house are not fully adequate to fulfill this ministry; the importance of the evangelical school must be reaffirmed."[40]

Henry, like Ockenga, considered education and the cultivation of the intellect as essential to the church's survival and ongoing witness in a modern world. The professor showed great concern in his chapter for the promotion of a theologically informed church even as he called for a concentrated apologetic. While the church's first order of business was the need to call his fellow believers to bolster their thought-program, they also needed "to press the Christian world-life view" upon non-Christians. Believers could not opt out of serious intellectual engagement because they had been saved by grace. On the contrary, they needed to ensure their schools met "the highest academic standards" in order to show the younger generation that Christianity afforded them "the only adequate spiritual ground." This meant the opening of several fronts that the church had largely neglected: writing a body of credible academic literature, teaching that engaged the great intellectual questions of the day, and the founding of institutions that could instantiate this perspective.

Ockenga's convocation address and Henry's bestselling book reveal both the intent and the program of the neo-evangelical effort to revitalize the Christian mind. Fuller Seminary, with Christian efforts more broadly, counted as the cornerstone of its mission the countering of non-Christian ideology. This labor, spurred on by a team of expert theologians adept in front of a class and in front of the typewriter, would drive all of the neo-evangelical program, whether preaching, missions work, evangelism, or social involvement. For the Cambridge evangelicals, head and heart worked in tandem, symbiotically, to produce a life that won glory to God and left a mark on a fallen world.

The faith did not melt away when challenged by non-Christians; the gospel did not pulverize one's intellectual faculties, rendering them mute in the face of secular argument. These Christians believed earnestly that Christianity allowed the mind to come alive, to flourish as the Creator had intended.

The drive to re-envision evangelicalism as an intellectually robust movement had now taken tangible shape. Its leaders had shown that such a project was no pipe dream. But Fuller was just a start. Several other noteworthy efforts began in this time as an outworking of the drive to renew the Christian mind, among them the Evangelical Theological Society and *Christianity Today* magazine. Their origin stories and early years show that the neo-evangelicals were not content with the formation of Fuller. They had a wider plan than that.

This plan began with the founding of the Evangelical Theological Society (ETS) in 1949. ETS grew out of the National Association of Evangelicals, which sponsored a series of academically oriented gatherings at its early national meetings.[41] Evangelical scholars soon realized that a national organization would aid in the advancement of scholarly evangelicalism. This burden took shape in an early document titled simply "*The Evangelical Theological Society*," which expressed "a sad confession": "Most Conservative scholars are painfully aware of the fact that most of the Biblical and theological literature which is being published these days, other than popular materials prepared especially for laymen, is Liberal in character." As a result, "Surely there is a very great need for Conservative men to publish Biblical and theological studies if we hope to influence in the right direction the religious thinking of the American people."[42] A new organization was needed.

The interested parties held an initial gathering in Cincinnati in December 1949 to discuss key evangelical topics. The press release for the event promised the kind of bold effort that characterized scholarly neo-evangelicalism more generally. The Evangelical Theological Society represented "a significant step on the part of Conservatives to present in a positive fashion the most fruitful results of evangelical scholarship and it is expected that its formation will have far reaching influence upon the theological thinking of the nation."[43] Of the Cambridge evangelicals, Henry and Merrill Tenney participated.

Henry was the keynote speaker of the first ETS meeting. He gave a message titled "Fifty Years of American Theology and the Contemporary Need." In his message, published later in the *Calvin Forum*, Henry called for distinctly Christian scholarship: *"We must also remember that our task is a scholarly task.* This is not an attempt to set scholarship over against piety. The two must ever go together. Their divorce is also one of the evils that much of modern scholarship has fostered. Genuine piety and true scholarship must ever go hand in hand." Henry quoted B. B. Warfield to strengthen his point: "Was it not Warfield who once wrote the beautiful sentence: 'The systematic theologian should ever rest on the bosom of his Redeemer'?

But my point now is that the task of us theologians in the proposed theological society is not one of preaching, of devotional stimulation, or of cultivation of the inner life, but primarily a task of scholarly endeavor."[44] ETS members heard the call, making quiet progress throughout the decade toward a more entrenched program. In 1958, ETS officially hit its stride with the publication of the *Bulletin of the Evangelical Theological Society*.[45]

The Cambridge evangelicals were by and large enthusiastic proponents of Henry's outlook. They played an important role in the early years of ETS. Tenney was the first vice-president of the association, and Ladd, Kuhn, Kantzer, Goddard, and Henry all served in leadership roles.[46] By 1952, Archer, Carnell, Ferrin, Lewis, Lindsell, Nicole, and Schultz had joined, with the result that the Boston scholars represented a significant percentage of the group's early members.[47] The organizing principle of ETS was the doctrine of biblical inerrancy. Undoubtedly the focus on this doctrine impeded certain evangelical attempts to penetrate the broader scholarly academy. However, coherence around this essential evangelical idea ensured that the organization, though fledgling in its first decade, had a core, a foundation, however mere this foundation may have been.

Many years later, Nicole reflected on this central tenet of the society: "The ETS was an effort to bring together people with differences of opinion on a number of things, but who were together on recognizing the authority of Scripture."[48] ETS in its early years was indeed home to numerous goals, methodologies, and plans for evangelical engagement in the broader academy. There was indeed a "sense of separateness" from nonevangelical scholars working in the same fields as ETS members.[49] Much work remained in order to accomplish the task at hand. ETS signaled, however, something of an early success story for the neo-evangelicals.

Other efforts to stimulate sound Christian thinking were less academic but more wide-ranging. In 1956, neo-evangelicals founded the magazine *Christianity Today*. As with Fuller Theological Seminary,

Carl Henry played a major role in this initiative, which began when Billy Graham drafted the initial vision for the magazine on a sleepless night in 1953. Graham remembered this occasion in his autobiography: "Trying not to disturb Ruth, I slipped out of bed and into my study upstairs to write. A couple of hours later, the concept of a new magazine was complete. I thought its name should be 'Christianity Today.'" The purpose of the magazine was expressly intellectual: "I wanted it also to be a focal point for the best in evangelical scholarship, for I knew that God was already beginning to raise up a new generation of highly trained scholars who were deeply committed to Christ and His Word."[50]

The intellectual ambition of this charter statement stands out, showing how pervasive the neo-evangelical drive to renew the Christian mind proved to be. Graham, an evangelist, wanted to renew the mind of evangelicalism's leaders. He wished for the magazine to showcase the "best in evangelical scholarship," a statement that reveals how widespread the pessimism over the Christian mind was in evangelical circles. Graham, contrary to popular opinion, did not want only spiritual revival of the heart. He wanted it to spread to the mind, and he wanted it to be clearly evangelical. The magazine, financed in large part by oilman J. Howard Pew, targeted pastors from a wide range of denominations, with an initial run of several hundred thousand issues reaching a national and international readership.[51] After a brief search, Graham tapped Henry as the periodical's first editor.[52]

Henry charted an ambitious course for the fledgling publication, drawing contributions from eminent theologians from both the American context and beyond. Many early iterations of the periodical boasted a table of contents like that on March 31, 1958, which featured the following essays: "The Bible View of Immortality" by Oscar Cullmann, "The Final Triumph" by Herman N. Ridderbos, and "The Intermediate State" by Johannes G. Vos.[53] The journal boasted similar lineups throughout its early years. Under Henry's careful oversight, *Christianity Today* (*CT*) flourished.

Such a work in such a climate meant that vitality would be hard won. The periodical faced the kinds of pressures endemic to such efforts—figuring out the exact nature of its funding base, answering questions about the specific mission and focus of the magazine, and untangling how Henry's role as editor meshed with his broader role as evangelical statesman. Henry felt stress from the beginning, writing in 1956 to board member Paul S. Rees that "[i]n the present circumstances, to lose one day from the office means to be utterly deluged with mail and other responsibilities." Health problems followed this pace. "Larry Ward and I have had complete physical check-ups in recent days," the editor wrote, "each feeling a heart ailment under the pressure of responsibilities from which there is no seeming relief."[54] Henry clearly chafed at the limits of his editorial role. He had too much energy and vision to sit in an office all day. He was an activist as much as a publisher.

Nevertheless, Henry was "heartened by the continuing subscription interest," which had reached twenty-seven thousand one month after the publication went to press.[55] An advertisement for the periodical eighteen months after its inception suggested that "CHRISTIANITY TODAY has achieved a widespread following in its relatively short life (18 months)."[56] Statistics followed: 46 percent of clergymen interviewed about their magazine of preference read *CT* "regularly" while 35 percent read it "occasionally." According to the release, these figures were higher than those for any other religious periodical in a major survey, including *The Christianity Century* and the *Christian Herald*.

From its early days, *CT* had an outsized influence in evangelical circles. On many matters, it both created and led discussion over a broad scope of theological and ecclesiological issues. *CT* never apologized during Henry's tenure for its doctrinal conservatism or for its aggressive interest in the biggest questions of the day, whether biblical, spiritual, doctrinal, cultural, political, or otherwise. Like all repositories of critical thought, the magazine regularly drew passionate responses and occasioned vigorous debate. In this early period of the periodical's existence, many considered *CT* an early success in advocating for the Christian worldview and in engaging challenges to the Christian faith on both an intellectual and spiritual level.

A scant two decades into their campaign to reposition doctrinally conservative American Protestantism, the neo-evangelicals, led by Ockenga, Henry, and Graham, had successfully established institutions that promoted their doctrinal and methodological viewpoint and won many adherents to their movement. The National Association of Evangelicals posited a new approach to cultural and social matters, the Graham crusades displayed a broadly appreciated and culturally friendly approach to evangelism, and Fuller Theological Seminary and *Christianity Today* advertised a resurgent intellectual program.

These efforts were driven by a fascinating coalition of popular preachers, big-time evangelists, and high-minded scholars. Rarely has such a diverse group of individuals, from an array of backgrounds, come together with such a unified focus. The radio homiletician Charles Fuller, the globe-trotting revivalist Billy Graham, the statesman-pastor Harold Ockenga, and the leading theologian Carl Henry all bought into the program. Something unusual developed in the 1940s as these and other leaders forged a common vision of intellectual presence in a secular culture. Complex as the beginnings of this venture were, however, sustaining it would prove more difficult indeed.

CHAPTER 6

CARL HENRY'S UNIVERSITY CRUSADE

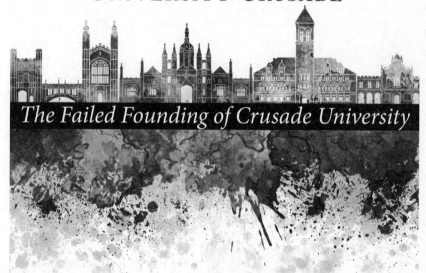

The Failed Founding of Crusade University

Carl F. H. Henry was nothing if not an ambitious Christian man. By the mid-1950s, he held two doctorates, was the dean of an upstart seminary that was the target of many a young would-be professor, and had written a book that sold tens of thousands of copies. He had the unique ability to speak in two languages: he could write for academics at the highest levels, critiquing Barth and chiding Brunner, and he could write for people in the pew, turning out a heart-warming devotional in an afternoon. Henry was a ceaseless whirl of activity, a force of nature, a literary figure to be reckoned with. Many years later, the catalogue of his books, articles, reviews, and essays is more than one hundred pages long and, at roughly thirty thousand words, is itself the length of a small book.

Henry was not a backslapper, though he was a prolific networker. He knew everyone in the evangelical world, and they knew him. He was generally warmhearted and wanted little more than for Christians to find common ground with one another and then minister together from that ground. His letters to friends and to the *Christianity Today* board reveal that he could be peevish at times; he was undoubtedly a man under pressure much of his life, whether from book due dates, journalistic deadlines, upcoming speaking engagements in far-flung locales, high-level movement crises needing his attention, and—always—the prospect of starting new works, new organizations, new institutions.

Henry was not ambitious for just anything, though. He wanted evangelicalism to own its theological identity. He certainly did in his own life; his interest in theological and philosophical material is evident in the copious notes and abbreviated sermon outlines he scratched out in the gospel of John in the well-worn Bible he preached from long after its binding disintegrated. His own major scholarly project centered in the question of epistemology and the Christian answer to this question, the doctrine of the Word. In order to jump-start the church's interest in theology, Henry became something of a one-man clearinghouse. He traveled all over the world speaking to churches and conferences. In his business suit and thick-rimmed glasses, he listened to lectures from leading thinkers and politicians when in Washington, DC, as the editor of the fledgling *Christianity Today* and then went home and pounded out reports. He approached the life of the mind with deadly seriousness. The human person was at stake in every battle of ideas. He dared to believe that his writing, speaking, and teaching could help win the battle.

But there was one project in particular that dazzled Henry, teased him, and long after it faded away as a realistic option, frustrated him. It was a great Christian research university, the undertaking that pulled his constellation of interests into one. In this project, his love for theology, education, cultural engagement, and the life of the mind met. If he and his peers could found such a school, their movement would be greatly strengthened, and the church would position itself to regain its long-lost cultural influence and intellectual gravitas.

It was not to be, of course. The drama of Henry's quest for this school—named Crusade University—is nonetheless revealing. It shows the strength of the ambition of the neo-evangelical thought-leaders, all of whom at one time were affiliated with or interested in this grand work. Ironically, it is in this failed effort that we most see just how unique Henry and his peers truly were among conservative Christians. They did not suffer from small dreams. They wanted not simply a new seminary, a new academic society, and a new journalistic outlet, all of which they formed in just a few short years. They wanted still more: an Ivy League–quality research university, the scholarly holy grail.

The drive to found a great Christian research institution began in the mid-1950s as many such ventures do: behind the closed doors of power brokers. Henry and Graham shared a conversation in 1955 that shaped the discussion of the project for years to come. This was a heady time for Graham. He had catapulted to megastardom several years earlier through his Los Angeles crusade, which drew the attention of newspaper magnate William Randolph Hearst.[1] Traveling all over the world, seeing thousands from all backgrounds come to Christ, Graham discovered a new ability to found institutions seemingly from nothing.[2]

Henry wrote to Graham on October 8, 1955, after the two had apparently talked some weeks before. Though Graham may have enthusiastically endorsed the idea early on, Henry quickly surpassed him in ardor and opinions. He called for an update on Graham's thinking: "[I]t is time, I think, for a first report on the matter of the Christian University, to which I have been giving considerable thought. Since I was pledged to confidence, I did not discuss it with Harold, but I have heard from several sources that the Boston area has a large hand in rejecting such a project, and this word has even reached the West Coast."[3] The "Harold" in question is Harold John Ockenga. Ockenga had served as a trustee of Gordon College for two decades and may have played a role in turning away possible schools from "the Boston area."

A Christian university of some sort seemed a foregone conclusion in 1955. Henry made mention of similar ideas held by other doctrinally conservative Protestants in the period: "Two somewhat similar Christian University projects are in the air . . . a federation of six colleges into seminaries as a Lutheran University of America, under a plan which would bring together the hundred fifteen faculty members on a single campus." Furthermore, "the idea of a Calvinistic University, which has been discussed on and off for 50 years, is again being renewed, this time by the Grand Rapids forces at Calvin College and seminary. This group has worked out a Protestant philosophy of education which it has projected a Christian grammar schools, high schools, Junior colleges and a senior college, as well as seminary, in Grand Rapids."[*] Henry promised to look into these matters, assuring Graham, "I shall write to inquire what locations are projected by these groups. I guess would be Minneapolis for the former [sic], Grand Rapids for the latter. For our venture, I would prefer the South, would you not?" The ideal location for the proposed school would shift many times over the years; it is likely that Henry chose the South because Graham was identified with it.

Henry saw fit at this point to propound his vision for the school. Of course, he hoped for Graham to adopt his vision and champion it. His letter reveals the careful attention Henry had given to conceptualizing the university. As his sketch reveals, Henry was a visionary thinker when it came to Christian engagement of the modern secular academy. His plans were grand and thorough:

> In two ways the Christian University we project must differ from the presently established evangelical universities . . . It must in no way be projected from the standpoint of offering those who attend these colleges an opportunity to pursue graduate studies leading to the doctorate without exposing them to the secular universities. To do that would be ruinous for us, for we are thinking of rectifying in improving the status quo rather than extending it. Therefore they do not provide for us the pattern of what we are after. They have not in

any significant way thrown themselves into the cultural crisis, but have abandoned the effective articulation of Christianity in relationship to the great cultural issues—education, economics, politics, art, and even theology—to the non-evangelical groups. Their passion has been evangelism, missions, and Christian education in the narrow sense, but not really Christian education in the large.[5]

Henry's analysis of the established evangelical academy resonates with material considered in earlier chapters, including Ockenga's 1947 Fuller convocation address and Henry's own *The Uneasy Conscience of Modern Fundamentalism*. Eight years after the publication and widespread dispersal of his book, Henry's fire for a vivified Christian intellect had not died. Believers found themselves in a "cultural crisis" that demanded "effective articulation" on "great cultural issues"—but none was forthcoming, as Henry saw it. The great questions of leading disciplines were still being asked, but Christians of the day did not possess the tools to answer them. The formation of a great school could rectify this problem, however.

In order to do so, the school had two major needs. The first dealt with curriculum, the second with faculty:

1. To provide an institution for preparing men professionally and for the pursuit of collegiate and post-collegiate studies leading to higher degrees, in an environment which so articulates evangelical Christianity in relationship to the cultural crisis in all the areas of study that we shall attract students who would otherwise be inclined to go to the big established universities such as Harvard, Yale, etc. this would be done notably broadly on the general collegiate base, but in a specialized way in the various schools, e.g., literature, philosophy, physical sciences, biological sciences, education, etc., the whole proceeding from an emphasis on the Christian concept of vocation.

2. Fundamental to the above is a faculty composed not merely of scholars who have at one time mastered the content of their field, and who have managed to wrest out a respectable PhD, but of men

> who are working up the Christian implications for contemporary
> issues in their field, I do recognize that University means a compa-
> ny of scholars seeking unanimity of conviction in the articulation
> of their convictions, and working earnestly together to forge a
> Christian alternative to the secular interpretations of our day, and
> who are dedicated to scholarly earnestness and production (not
> to outside preaching), restless to supply textbooks in the various
> spheres of study, and thus productive of students who are fired by
> the same devotion to scholarship and research (the future Augus-
> tines and Anselms and Calvins). I shall have something to say at a
> later date about some of these potential faculty members.[6]

Henry wished for the college in question to serve as a launching pad,
not an endpoint, for bright young Christians. As discussed in previous
chapters, some evangelicals and many fundamentalists retreated from
higher education in the first half of the twentieth century, viewing
modern academia with suspicion. Many sought undergraduate credentials from in-house, movement-driven personalities and stopped
there. Henry had the opposite vision. He wished to "attract students"
from none other than Harvard and to educate them with excellence in
a curriculum grounded in "the Christian concept of vocation," in oppo-
sition to the traditional Bible college curriculum, which one might say
was grounded in the Christian concept of salvation. Of course, Henry
likely would have noticed that taking top evangelical students out of
elite schools would remove leaven from the dough, but he no doubt
believed that the gains outweighed the losses in such a situation.

The Fuller theologian also urged Graham to seek none but the
very best and most productive Christian scholars in "various spheres
of study." Henry wanted not merely those who had proven able "to
wrest out a respectable PhD," but those who had mastered their field
and saw themselves as scholars. Henry did not denigrate preaching in
any sense, but he did believe that "outside preaching" would detract
from the work of creating a uniquely Christian worldview and the
literature that would undergird it. Henry likely knew well the lines of

tension he walked; doubtless it was of great benefit to many schools and students that many evangelical professors ministered in local churches. He wished for pure scholars, however, academicians who were essentially of the same caliber as Ivy League professors, but were resolute Christians. This brief description of the ideal faculty member, of course, fits what Henry himself sought to do in his own academic career and what many of the Cambridge evangelicals likewise pursued.

Graham responded to Henry's letter promptly. He mentioned various conversations with cultural leaders, all of whom indicated support of the idea:

> I have been giving a great deal of thought to the University project. I had a long talk with Harold Ockenga and John Bolten about it. They are extremely enthusiastic. I also talked with VP Nixon, Mr. Sid Richardson, and several other prominent people, including Gov. Dewey and Mr. DeWitt Wallace of Reader's Digest. They all feel that there is a definite need in this field. It seems also the feeling of all that I have discussed it with that this University should be definitely in the East, preferably New England. Or something about an Eastern University that has a different prestige, it seems, and one in the West area. This may be entirely wrong, but at least it seems to be the opinion of Harold and others.[7]

Ockenga, Graham reported, had at this point suggested that Gordon College might serve as the site of the new school:

> Harold Ockenga feels that Gordon might be the place to build, since they already have a beautiful campus and at least a beginning. He is entirely agreed that it must be a top university from the opening here. He is very anxious that you and I, he and John and others get together and have a talk about it. I told him that you and I had first discussed it and prayed together. He said this had been on his heart for many years.
>
> They have elected me as a trustee of Gordon, though this has no

direct bearing on the University project. Harold said that they would
be willing to change the name of Gordon and start from scratch again,
or he would be just as interested if we decided Abbey University be
in some other part of the country. I do not think he has any personal
ambition in this direction, only has a very heavy burden about it and
would like to see the project carried through.[8]

Graham had the opportunity to speak to some of the most powerful people in America about the school and did. Despite the fact that
most Christians in America hailed from the South, many thought the
school best located in the academic Northeast, including Ockenga,
who adored New England and its intellectual bent. John Bolten, the
financier of the Plymouth Scholars' conferences, indicated interest in
the project. Ockenga, though not the president of Gordon College,
conveyed to Graham that Gordon could "start from scratch," a
remarkable suggestion. According to Graham, Ockenga did not wish
to lead the school but only wanted to see the project happen. In the
very early stages of this idea, many of the pieces to the puzzle were
in place.

Henry wrote to Graham a day later, though he had not received
Graham's reply. He noted in an exhilarated tone that he had just "gotten a surprising word that you join [sic] the Gordon board, and that
a new Christian University is being projected in New England with
Gordon as the base, and that you will be throwing your influence
and resources behind it."[9] He called this "almost incredible" and a
"strategical blunder." Henry urged "procurement of the necessary
funds" instead of rushing the idea. At this stage in the drive to create
a stellar Christian research university, it is not difficult to peg Henry
as the principled curator of the project and Graham as the breezy
entrepreneur. The two men operated from different positions from
the inception of the plan, with Henry straining valiantly to make it
happen and Graham exercising either high-flown creativity or judicious remove at different times.[10]

Henry shifted his tone, sounding mildly alarmed. "The real issue," he told his evangelist friend, "is the fact that such a strategy would blunt the edge of the new and vigorous approach to an evangelical philosophy of education which we so desperately need, and which the present universities lack the insight and vitality to practice. In my previous letter about this. . . I indicated some of these elements."[11] Henry then expanded upon his contention, stated earlier, that the school needed a superstructure that would allow it to transcend many of the difficulties that smaller educational ventures faced. Speaking with awareness of his decided interest in the project, he confessed to Graham that he would "probably frighten you when I speak now about what is needed really to do the job in a proper manner." He unfolded his plans:

> The first, and easiest, and indispensable step, is the establishment of a liberal arts college, with all the related departments (e.g., languages, sciences, philosophy, history, social sciences, etc.). With sufficient faculty strength to offer degrees in these spheres right up through the doctorates. My impression is that to project buildings, administration, faculty, equipment and other needs, such a venture would involve an investment of $100 million. The present Harvard endowment is 350 million.
>
> The next step would be the addition of colleges other than liberal arts. Of these, two were the easiest to add—the college of education, and the college of business administration, in that order. Those more difficult to add would be such colleges as engineering, law, medicine, etc., although if a great Christian University were projected, they could not permanently be ignored.
>
> The overall venture, if I may express an initial procession, would require some $300 million, which. . . would include sufficient endowment to guarantee its operation.[12]

Henry closed by pointing out that Graham, slated to meet with John D. Rockefeller Jr. in coming weeks, could raise the prospect of the university with the Standard Oil scion. Here Henry's lasting preference for the site of the school emerged: "[T]he fact that his father once selected a specific site in New York City (near Gramercy Park) for such University, the impression grows that New York City would not, after all, be an unhappy location."[13] New York was regarded as the center of the world, at least in symbolic terms. This was not lost on Henry, nor was school's need of a New York–level financier. The theologian, after all, was thinking broadly about the school. In fact, he could scarcely have thought *more* ambitiously. He wanted a top-notch liberal arts, a college of education, another of business administration, and more if the investors could handle them. His projected endowment was $300 million, a mind-boggling sum for the evangelical world and most any other context.

The idea percolated. Conversations continued among the major players and others who professed interest. At one point, Henry enjoyed a correspondence with John H. Strong, son of Baptist theologian Augustus Hopkins Strong, who communicated enthusiasm for the project.[14] Henry later relayed the exchange to Graham and noted how much Strong appreciated the evangelist. There was a historic dimension to this contact, Henry thought; the senior Strong had "enlisted Mr. Rockefeller Senior's support for the idea of a Christian University while pastor of the Rockefeller church in Cleveland," though the plan soon collapsed.[15] Perhaps, mused Henry, things might turn out more auspiciously in their day. For a time, however, the project went quiet.

Several years later, in November 1959, it flared to life. A number of high-profile evangelical leaders and educators met at the Statler Hotel in Washington, DC, on December 29, 1959. The group formally met to discuss "Crusade University" and included Dr. Billy Graham, chairman Dr. David Baker, Mr. Henderson Belk, Dr. L. Nelson Bell, Mr. Howard Butt Jr., Mr. George Champion, Dr. Enoch Dyrness, Dr. V. Raymond Edman, Mr. Logan Fulrath, Mr. Carl Gunderson, Mr. Paul Harvey, Roger Hull, Maxey Jarman, Mr. Stanley Kresge, Senior, Mr. William Mead, Dr. Harold Ockenga, Dr. Stephen Payne, Mr. J. Howard Pew, Mr. C. A. Pitts, Dr. Daniel Poling, Mr. Jacob Stam, and Rev. Grady Wilson.[16] Several months before the precipitous meeting, Graham and Henry had sent out a special booklet titled "A Time for Decision in Higher Education: Billy Graham Presents Crusade University." The cover featured Graham flashing his dazzling smile and included an inscription from 1 Samuel 12:23, "I will teach you the good... way" (KJV).[17] The booklet offers the best glimpse of any document of the ambitions of the evangelicals who wished to start a Christian university.

The booklet first identified the need for a great Christian research university. It covered demographic changes in America, identified straightforwardly as a "Christian nation," then moved on to the spiritual "crisis" in the country:

> In recent years attention has been focused on our population growth and the swelling enrollments in elementary and secondary schools. The effects will soon be felt in our colleges and universities, many of which are already overtaxed. Current estimates, based on population trends, indicate the college enrollments are likely to double in the next 10 years.
>
> The crisis in higher education is being studied on state and national levels, and all agreed that it will take the united effort of private and tax supported institutions to meet the challenge. In the past there has been a wholesome balance in the field of higher education between privately endowed institutions and state-supported schools. Already the balance is being upset and unless existing private schools are enlarged in [sic] additional privately endowed colleges are established in the next few years, the function of training our young people will of necessity be largely taken over by the state.
>
> Although a Christian nation, our Supreme Court has ruled that the Bible may not be taught in tax-supported institutions. As Christians, we believe that the Bible still holds the solution to man's age-old problems of life and that it should have its rightful place in the training of our young people.
>
> This brochure has been prepared in the hope that it may stimulate

action on the part of those who are in a position to help solve the critical problem facing higher education and more particularly the problem of thousands of earnest young people seeking a Christian higher education.[18]

The booklet played off of common evangelical fears about the encroachment of the state even as it called attention to the lack of biblical training in public institutions. The text does not reflect the insights Henry proffered in his letter to Graham; missing here is a fulsome description of the need for an integrative, worldview-oriented philosophy of all things. The copy more plainly calls for the stimulation of "a Christian higher education." Such boilerplate descriptions of the school's purpose and function were likely malleable in this period. Nonetheless, Henry's shimmering intellectual imagination is missing from the booklet's copy.

The school had multiple "objectives," several of which signify a more ambitious program. Crusade University sought several goals:

> To provide the highest academic training in the liberal arts and selected professional areas for men and women, with a view to training Christian leaders.
>
> To present the Christian theistic view of the world, of man, and of man's culture in the light of biblical and natural revelation.
>
> To present the Bible as the word of God, with emphasis on its absolute validity.
>
> To offer areas of concentration in the liberal arts in such professional areas as may be selected.
>
> To seek to develop habits of Christian citizenship which will enable the student to participate constructively in the life of his community and to recognize his responsibility to the needs of the world.
>
> To assure physical well-being in a wholesome Christian personality by encouraging student participation in spiritual, social, and recreational activities.
>
> To offer graduate training in theology and such other areas of

specialization as will contribute to the well-being of mankind, as rapidly as such programs can be soundly developed.[19]

The school's objectives include more of the kind of educational theorizing offered by Henry to Graham, and there is evidence of the theologian's influence in such phrases as "the Christian theistic view of the world," the "absolute validity" of the Word, and the need for young believers to acknowledge their "responsibility to the needs of the world." The school as charted here displays a preference for the "liberal arts," suggesting that the founders believed that a classical education would better prepare students for redemptive service in the world than the kind of program offered by many fundamentalist schools, which in many places meant classes in the Bible and practical ministry. The visionaries behind Crusade University championed the need to address and work within the broader culture of the country. Ideally, a graduate of the university would "participate constructively in the life of his community" and work for "the well-being of mankind."

Such language signals a shift from the mindset of previous generations of believers, who focused more on their own communities. The booklet, printed on fine paper and featuring color renderings of the subjects in question—students, buildings, faculty—moved to more esoteric matters. The question of "Control" surfaced next. "The control of the University will be vested in a self-perpetuating board of trustees of 20 members, elected for a five-year term (four to be elected each year). Each member of the board will subscribe to the doctrinal statement of the University and will be dedicated to the cause of Christian education."[20]

Perhaps the most noteworthy feature of this projected effort is that its doctrinal statement, as per usual for the neo-evangelicals, bound them to no one denomination or group. Like the National Association of Evangelicals, Fuller Theological Seminary, and *Christianity Today* magazine, Crusade University would be interdenominational. This orientation freed the school up to work across traditional boundary markers and to promote a pan-Christian identity. It also presented difficulties inherent in such coalitional work, namely, agreement on such seemingly abstruse matters as the school's code of conduct, a question which soon became a quagmire.

The booklet next treated the ideal "Location" of the school, suggesting that it take roots in New Jersey. Apparently, Henry's view had won the day, though he had not succeeded at this point in landing the school in the cultural nucleus, New York City:

> After a careful study of the various areas of the country, it appears that a site in New Jersey as close to New York City as possible would be desirable. A number of factors have entered into this consideration, including the fact that New Jersey has relatively few colleges and universities. In the fall of 1958, the total enrollment in all New Jersey institutions amounted to only 66% of the young people from that state enrolled in college. The advantages of being near a large city such as New York are evident. In addition to the educational opportunities, it would afford convenient transportation facilities for the many students who would be coming from a distance.[21]

The booklet, rife with the latest statistical information, made the case for a mid-Atlantic location by pointing out that New Jersey had "relatively few colleges and universities." In other words, the neo-evangelicals could make a splash by founding a university in the state. The advantages of moving to New York City were obvious; the city was the country's most significant urban center. Two years earlier, Graham conducted a landmark crusade in the city, preaching to more than two million people, seeing roughly fifty-five thousand respond to his message, and making national headlines for weeks.[22] One newspaper called the event "the high point" of the evangelist's already stratospheric career.[23] Graham himself remembered that "New York also had an unforeseen impact on our own ministry."

Television played a large part in this impact: "[A]n estimated 96 million people had seen at least one of the meetings from Madison Square Garden," according to the preacher, which "resulted in a flood of invitations to other major cities under broad sponsorship, including Chicago."[24] The pantheon of postwar evangelical leaders would not have missed the outsized effect of an effort in New York City, or at least near it. The city was cutting-edge, exploding in population, and perfectly suited to a generation of Christian leaders who brimmed with grand plans of cultural influence.

The faculty, a subject of discussion in the Henry-Graham correspondence, came up next. Above a picture of three formally dressed men and three women around a table, the copy read that "Christian teachers with the best training obtainable will be sought for the various departments. Men of proven ability and experience will had [*sic*] the departments and schools, and will be asked to take an active part in recruiting their own staffs."[25] Inasmuch as was possible, "those with a PhD or equivalent training will be sought for the teaching staff." The booklet hedged a bit on the matter of whether doctorate-earning faculty would teach at Crusade University. The language of the faculty statement was still strong but less convicted of the need for credentials than Henry.

The "Suggested campus plan" showed three long rectangular quads with two major buildings at each end of the quads. Dormitories faced one another in the middle of the quads. The entire campus was connected by walkways; a major football stadium was located in the background. The plan was not especially ornate or inventive but evinced a crisp, sensible layout. The sports stadium, long a subject of university discussion over the role of athletics in relation to academics in the mission of the college, showed that the neo-evangelicals did not merely desire lab-coated scientists and future engineers in business suits.

What would the cost of tuition be for students, and faculty salaries? Graham's booklet next laid out its stance on these important matters: "The faculty salaries will be above average, though not the highest since it is felt that the teachers employed should be those who are dedicated to the cause of Christian education and who are more interested in serving Christ than in earning a large salary. They will not, however, be asked to sacrifice financially in order to teach at the University."[26]

The would-be founders projected generous salaries for faculty members. The board wished to draw both a wide-ranging student body and an accomplished faculty. Faculty members bearing the rank of "Professor" who taught such small classes could expect a nine-month salary of twelve thousand dollars, which compared favorably with the median average of eight thousand dollars for this rank. The total budget allotted for all seventy professors and other educational personnel (library, administration, and so on) was $803,000. The total operating budget for Crusade would be $1,275,000.[27] The initial investment needed for the school's endowment was five million dollars; the overall investment for the school's operating costs was over eighteen million dollars. This was a far cry from the three hundred million dollars Henry sought, but it was undoubtedly a more realistic figure for the day.

The booklet closed with the projected costs of Crusade University. Henry mentioned the "brochure" in a "Report to the Steering Committee" of the proposed school sent two weeks before the meeting in DC. He cited Graham as the instigator for a new school and urged serious consideration of the proposal in order to move things forward: "When Billy Graham first mentioned this project to me, I immediately suggested the possibility of achieving his objectives by means of the second alternative outlined in paragraph B.[28] However, it seemed clear to him that a completely new institution would be preferable. Each existing institution has its own objectives and distinctive characteristics, and I am inclined to feel that this burden was laid on Billy's heart by the Lord for a definite purpose."

Henry added his own strong commendation of this suggestion: "Although there is undoubtedly room in our country for more conservative theological training centers, the need for evangelical training in other fields of leadership is in some respects even greater. We should, therefore, do what we can to train able leaders for such fields as diplomacy, business, teaching, and other key professions as well as the ministry."[29] Henry publicly committed himself to the promotion of the great evangelical university. Though anchored in the ministry world, he nonetheless expressed a strong desire to serve the evangelical cause by developing a wide range of leaders who would serve in "key professions" like politics, business, and education.

The venture would not happen so easily. When the parties came together in December 1959, they enjoyed a vigorous discussion over its nature and vision.[30] The committee chaired by David Baker and helmed by Graham had much before them to consider—who to hire, how to fund the school, where exactly to locate it. These and numerous other issues promised to affect the very nature of the institution, which was a precarious proposition at best. An interdenominational committee composed of figures representing existing schools, all of which had their own major needs and goals, considered the establishing of a university linked to no major denomination (and thus no one institutional funding source, or confession) that would, if formed, lead to the plundering of many of the top faculty members from Christian schools and the removal of many Christian scholars from secular environments. A tall order, this.

The effort would depend on the generosity of several donors, each of whom would have a vested and possibly meddling interest in the school. Yet this highly complex situation carried great promise as well. The promotion of the kind of robust theological worldview championed by Ockenga, the Cambridge evangelicals, and the neo-evangelicals more broadly would have a home, and not merely one designed to prepare ministers, significant as Fuller was.

The first meeting of the parties interested in Crusade University produced what so many such meetings do: committees. Little in the way of a decisive vision was reached, however. What was more, the board found that it did not agree on the matter of campus standards or the student moral code. In light of such weighty priorities as funding, location, and faculty, this subject may seem quixotic. Yet it engaged the group like no other detail. Discussions spilled over into the summer and led to a second meeting in the fall. In the meantime, attention accrued to the effort. An article by John McCandless Phillips titled "Protestants Map University Here" appeared in none other than the *New York Times*.[31] Phillips noted in his subtitle on page A5 that "Dr. Graham favors" the idea and reported that "a decision on the project is expected this summer." The initial investment needed would be "about $20,000,000."[32]

Henry used his own bully pulpit in *Christianity Today* to make the public case for the Christian university, a subject that caused no small amount of feedback among a constituency that enjoyed loyalty to many different Christian schools, all of which would be affected by a major new Christian research institution. In October 1960, Henry published his piece, which suggested provocatively that no elite Christian school existed: "It is not proposed to set up just another Christian college (or University, and the larger view) but a University *of the highest academic excellence.* This need is not filled by existing institutions." The university Henry proposed would be distinct, "dedicated not only to the Faith but also to the highest and most rigorous academic standards.... At the core, solid, dynamic Christian unity; in the branches, solid and creative scholarship."[33]

This was a bold statement to make in the Christian public square. Alumni from schools like Wheaton, Gordon, and Biola read the flagship evangelical magazine and would not necessarily have assumed that their alma mater did not represent academic excellence. Henry brooked no compromise in his views, however. He wanted the school to be grounded in "Christian unity" and producing the strongest "creative scholarship" such that "the secular world" would have to reckon with it. No such university existed, though a "very few" institutions had earned "well-deserved respect." As an educational theorist, Henry was no less shy than he was as a theologian.

Henry then covered territory that would have raised hackles for some of his readers, particularly those who carried a latent distrust for modern scholarship. He made an apology for a decidedly academic mindset, arguing that such was necessary for the production of excellent academic labor:

> [W]e may at least suggest a part of it by speaking of that sometimes bewildering thing, the "scholarly mentality." (Remember, now, we are speaking of Christian *education*, not Christian evangelism.) That mentality demands a very specific kind of environment. Among the lesser things it demands are scholarly facilities (such as libraries and laboratories), the companionship of other dedicated scholars, encouragement by the administration of independent research, challenging and intellectually competent students, graduate-level teaching. But above all else it demands *intellectual freedom*.[34]

Henry had to attempt some serious intellectual footwork in order to avoid losing many of his hearers who prioritized evangelism. Some would have heard Henry as saying that education, not evangelism, was important. The traditional evangelical focus on evangelism was sufficiently strong that it was possible for Henry's audience to hear a call for the kind of academic engagement provided by a research university as a diversion from first things, namely, the publishing of the gospel abroad. Henry knew of this difficulty in translation but forged ahead, calling the evangelical public to get behind a range of academic needs that would cohere in the school in question, including appropriate academic facilities, high-level teaching, and especially "intellectual freedom."

Henry's editorial drew a mixed response. Some readers loved it; others expressed concerns. The issue remained on the table for some months until prospective founders of Crusade University met again on November 4–5, 1960. Those in attendance were Billy Graham (host); Dr. Ronald C. Doll, School of Education, New York University; Dr. Enoch C. Dyrness, registrar, Wheaton College; Dr. Lars I. Granberg, Department of Psychology, Hope College; Dr. W. Harry Jellema, Department of Philosophy, Calvin College; Dr. Harold Lindsell, Dean, Fuller Theological Seminary; Dr. Calvin D. Linton, Dean of Colombian

College, George Washington University; Dr. C. Gregg Singer, Department of History, Catawba College; Dr. Orville S. Walters, Director of Health Services, University of Illinois; Dr. C. Stacy Woods, General Secretary, International Fellowship of Evangelical Scholars.[35] Henry presided over the meeting.

Discussion waxed hot on the matter of behavioral standards. It is clear from the minutes that nothing so drove conversation at the Statler as student morality. The following is a selection from an expansive discussion of the topic that allows us to see the give-and-take, and diversity of opinion, operative in the discussion:

1. "I look upon the inculcation of some of these personal habits not so much as a matter of morality as an opportunity for discipline" (Graham). The students at West Point are brought under a very rigid code, and this is later reflected for all their lives. We could ask for strict personal discipline against alcohol, tobacco (though be more open in respect to movies). The people who cracked up under communist pressures in Korea had no firmly held standards (Doll). Why not require spiritual discipline—up at 5 AM for an hour of prayer—rather than vacations (Henry)?

2. Why single out particular items for moral condemnation (e.g., drinking, smoking, gambling)?
   (i.) It is easy to condemn others for devices for which we have no taste ourselves, what of gluttony, intellectual laziness, lovelessness? (Linton).
   (ii.) In our (Christian reformed) circles, reading the Sunday papers is looked upon with disapproval (Jellema); in some places in Europe, we had asked crusade workers to forgo the use of lipstick because it was regarded as worldly (Graham); some Nazarenes object to jewelry for the same reason, etc. such prejudices are often parochial, and not universally shared moral judgments.
   (iii.) Machen: when a group forbids what God allows, its next step is to allow what God forbids (Singer).

This material is only a small swatch of the broader conversational fabric. Though the tone is polite throughout, it is clear that the discussion drew passionate opinions from many of the group's members. Dyrness, Granberg, and Walter represented the strongest proponents of a rigorous moral code; Jellema, Singer, and Woods generally opposed such a practice. Graham and Henry attempted to toe the line in committee, though Graham seemed to lean toward the right (the more conservative side), Henry to the left.

The discussion reveals the seriousness with which evangelicals, for better and for worse, took campus standards. More than any other matter recorded in the minutes, this topic occupied the committee. Several reasons account for the vigorous debate. First, many of the discussants had grown up in fundamentalist or highly conservative churches. Second, even expressly "evangelical" colleges of the period had stringent moral codes. Not to have such a behavioral guide would have seemed "liberal" or "progressive" to Christians for whom these labels indicated theological and personal compromise. Indeed, many schools of the liberal Christian tradition had indeed modified or scuttled codes of morality; certainly the broad sweep of colleges and universities founded for the purpose of Christian instruction had done so. Third, the issue truly did merit attention. Would a school merely "suggest" what Christian behavior was appropriate or, looser still, leave the matter up to students? If Crusade was going to train students to live passionate lives of Christian service, how would it connect the ethics taught in classes to their personal walk with Christ?

For his part, Henry weighed in substantially in the debate with a blistering paper. Though he explicitly stated that "a place must be found for specific standards on a college campus, provided only that the philosophy of conduct be properly elaborated," he offered strong critique of the traditional evangelical philosophy behind campus behavioral codes. Henry, who had just authored a book titled *Christian Personal Ethics*,[36] suggested that "[t]he essence of Christian personal ethics lies in the possession of positive virtues, not in the near avoidance of evils. To equate 'the separated life' swiftly with avoidance is to devalue the biblical virtues, such as love, joy, peace, long-suffering, kindness, goodness, self-control, and so forth."

Evangelical holiness was for Henry more about obedience to scriptural teaching than an extra-biblical code: "The life of sanctification ought to be identified by God's people primarily in terms of biblical criteria, rather than by a requirement of details of Christian behavior for which there exists no direct biblical mandate."[37] As crops up so often in the writing of Henry, the Boston scholars, and their fellow neo-evangelicals, this argument shows a distaste for what one could call a "simple separationism." Though the discharging of a strong biblical ethic would in fact necessitate "avoidance of certain social practices," the core of the ethical life was "the possession of positive virtues" such as those found in Galatians 5:22–23, which Henry quoted without citation. Henry viewed the definition of ethics as merely the "boycotting" of certain practices as immature and unformed.

Like much of Henry's thinking and writing, this was a nuanced position. Nuance played well in Henry's classrooms. It did not play as well in a discussion of campus standards, which tended to draw strong assertions, even condemnations, from all sides. There is perhaps bitter irony in the reality that while the committee reached relatively easy unanimity on a doctrinal statement, it was a morality code—whether to forbid smoking, card-playing, and going to movies—that halted what existing momentum the task-force shared.

This was not the only material Henry shared at the meeting. He strongly urged the committee not to develop the school in question as a Bible school. He preferred the establishment of a research school, which in his view held "highest priority on the list of needs if we are to achieve a decisive evangelical "breakthrough" at the educational level." Henry walked through a number of topics on this matter before hitting his stride in a discussion of what the school's image should be. This statement, worth quoting at length, sums up much of the views quoted heretofore in this chapter and offers a powerful expression of Henry's bold idea:

> More important than all considerations of "where and when," however, is the basic matter of the image of this University and the academic world. Such a school, if worthy of its purpose, must with thought and life at their highest levels in the rich context of the Bible. It must be (1) evangelical in urgency, (2) evangelical in doctrine, (3) committed to academic standards and moral purity—but, unless it is much more also it cannot generally qualify as a Christian University. Such an institution will not be too greatly interested in "the reputation of numbers," but (4) will honor the importance of personal academic relationships between professors and students, and will guard even underclassmen from exposure to faculty novices. Its qualified teachers must be concerned for (5) the unification of all the university disciplines in the interest of a Christian world-life view which integrates the whole of life's experiences area with an eye on tragic cultural crises of our times, they must (6) set forth the political, economic and social applications of Christianity, and thus expound a consistent criticism of an alternative to socialistic revisions of the social order. Beyond a deep sense of personal devotion to the Lord, the faculty must (7) grasp the history of thought and systematic orientation to Jesus Christ as the revealed center of history, nature, conscience and redemption, by bringing the "ancient mind," the "medieval mind," the "modern mind," the "contemporary mind" under the judgment of divine revelation; besides interest simply in personal projects and literary excursions, such a faculty must be ready to (8) engage in corporate conversation, research and writing, each making some minimal contribution for the production of textbooks that will enable the evangelical enterprise to challenge the initiative of secular scholars, and to penetrate the collegiate world. It is [sic] such a university is really to rise to its greatest potential, in its necessary dedication to evangelical standards of doctrine of life, it will seek also to (9) provide a platform for the ablest evangelical scholars of all traditions, in order to solidify the interdenominational, international witness of conservative Christianity.[38]

Henry's statement amounted to his in-person magnum opus on the question of the Christian research university. Never again would he so vividly capture the unique prospect of a school like Crusade University, which he saw as a vital part of the "interdenominational, international witness of conservative Christianity." Henry did not merely wish for the school's professorate to profess faith in Jesus Christ as savior; he wanted the brightest evangelical minds to conceptualize Christ as "the revealed center of history, nature, conscience and redemption." Henry wanted professors to teach every subject as if Jesus Christ really was the alpha and omega, the beginning and the end of all things.

This committee statement got lost in the shuffle, and it has never seen the light of day. It demonstrates, though, Henry's ability to think innovatively and theologically about a subject of great potential and importance. The committee broke in early November, the players returning to their ministries, pondering the prospects and perils of a venture like Crusade University. Henry, who had done so much to stimulate conversation at the meeting, made little mention of the proceedings until nearly two years later. In a letter to Dr. S. H. Mullen in September 1962, Henry sketched what had happened in the two years since the board meeting: "[S]ome 20,000 young people of college aged [*sic*] made personal commitments to Christ during the [1957] Madison Square Garden crusade of Billy Graham, and they were now, as it were, to be 'thrown to the wolves' so far as their collegiate learning was concerned in as much as there was no Christian college in the New York area that had full accreditation."[39] The failure to establish the university had resulted in many college students falling prey to modernism, in Henry's view.

The problems with the establishment of Crusade University were not limited to those suggested by Henry. The school had trouble enlisting help from major donors like John Bolten, who financed many of Ockenga's projects, including Fuller Theological Seminary, and J. Howard Pew, whose money drove efforts like Grove City College and *Christianity Today*. Many of the wealthiest evangelicals had long-standing ties with other schools; Garth Rosell has shown that though Bolten initially had interest in funding a university, he eventually lost interest due in part to a concern that secular schools would lose what little evangelical leaven they then had.[40] It may have been such lack of interest that allowed the project to crash on the rocks of the campus morality code. That is, perhaps if the major players—both financiers and statesmen like Graham—had felt stronger about the effort, the division over behavior might have mended itself. Daniel Poling, son of one of the men around the meeting table in 1960, later wrote that Graham's businessmen backers bet strongly against the project and advised him accordingly.[41] They saw it as a potential quagmire for a man whose career had taken off like a rocket.

Other problems arose as well. Henry wrote to William Schmidt Jr. in November 1962 and suggested that "[w]hile there remains a good deal of interest in the matter of a Christian University, the question of location is still as indefinite as ever—if not more so—and the matter has not moved to a point where any decision in this area is likely to be made in the immediate future."[42] Three years later, Henry appealed to Graham again, seeking to resuscitate the idea that once captivated their conversation.[43] Graham did not respond to Henry with any definite direction. He had been willing to entertain and even promote the idea in past years, but he had never approached the prospect of a research school with Henry's zeal. Graham clearly valued evangelical education and had given generously of his time to schools like Fuller. He had, moreover, served as a college president for a number of years. What ardor he once had for the project appears to have cooled, however.

Unlike his friend, Henry continued his quest. He responded to detractors, attempted to rally leading evangelicals, and presented his pitch to potential donors. In a letter written in August 1965, he laid out the possibilities of such a school, observing that "for 10 years and more some of us have been contemplating the possibility of a great Christian University, located near one of America's major cities accessibly to a major airport in nearby facilities of a large prestigious secular campus."[44] The promise of an excellent university was still great: "The pervasive scientific skepticism calls for a dedicated cadre of young intellectuals thoroughly grounded in evangelical perspectives, equipped to challenge alien views, and trained to penetrate and permeate the secular institutions of our age."[45]

Henry then suggested possible donations that could reverse this trend: first, the school could use twenty-five million dollars for a campus, liberal arts college, and graduate schools of "education, theology, communicative and creative arts, and philosophy." Second, if such a sum was too great, an interested party could contribute ten million dollars for a "Christian Institute of Advanced Studies" that might "subsequently become the graduate core of a Christian University. This estimate is predicated on $1 million for purchase and development of a graduate research center and library located within 15 or 20 min. of a prestigious university campus (Harvard, Princeton, Stanford, Chicago, Pennsylvania or Pittsburgh)."[46]

The Institute for Advanced Christian Studies (IFACS) begin its work in 1967. Led by Henry, it sought "to enunciate the Christian world-view in order to contain the secular tide that engulfs contemporary culture."[47] The project began promisingly, with directors from Indiana University, the University of Michigan, the Massachusetts Institute of Technology, and the University of Illinois.[48] Henry was the fifth inaugural director and the engine behind the Institute until it was shuttered in 2002.[49]

As Henry had indicated to Bell, the Institute attempted to locate itself in a major academic setting but could not. This did not prevent the organization from staging numerous conferences and sponsoring multiple projects by a pantheon of leading evangelical scholars over the next several decades. Recipients included Samuel Moffett, who wrote a two-volume work on the history of Christianity in Asia that anticipated the later explosion of academic interest in the Asian church; Nicholas Wolterstorff, who wrote on a Christian philosophy of art; and Ronald Sider, who worked on an apparently never-completed text on the resurrection of Christ in light of modern historical methodology.[50] Directors of IFACS over the years included historian Nathan Hatch and philosopher Ronald Nash. In his autobiography, Henry noted that IFACS had "funded 24 of 57 applications" for project funding with the median grant being six thousand dollars, a very generous sum for scholarly Christian work.[51] Much of the funding for the program came from the Lilly Endowment, though grants from outfits like the Billy Graham Evangelistic Association also enabled Henry's program to play a role in advancing the next generation of evangelical scholarship.[52]

As of March 1967, IFACS had begun. The quest for a great Christian research university continued apace, however, for Henry. He had corresponded with Ockenga one year earlier about the idea of locating the school in Amarillo, Texas, and had gone so far as to talk to Graham about it. In February 1966, he reported to the pastor that Graham worried that they "would run into direct hostility from Southern Baptists in that area that while funds might be available from some sources, this advantage would be outweighed by the hostility of the Southern Baptists, since their enthusiasm should be conserved if the University were located elsewhere."[53] Another possible launching pad cropped up in April 1966 when Wheaton president Hudson T. Armerding proposed a "national university composed of cooperating regionally accredited Christian liberal arts colleges."[54] Henry spoke kindly of the idea but noted that "there is a great deal more that can and needs to be done—and could be done."[55] This would mean something grander than the confederation Armerding proposed.

Against all the odds, the quest went on. A meeting in August 1968 at the Seven Continents restaurant at O'Hare Airport considered the possibility of a "cluster college campus" in the Pacific Northwest. In the proposal for the idea, the presidents of several colleges announced that "After three years of operation in the associated Christian colleges of Oregon, George Fox and Warner Pacific are ready to implement this new concept in Christian higher education."[56] Quaker theologian D. Elton Trueblood spoke at the meeting, which seemed like many such affairs to inspire initial interest in the idea, but Henry did not involve himself in such a plan in future days.

Henry's pursuit of the Christian university persisted into the 1980s when he was in his seventies. Henry was asked to give a presentation in June 1983 at the Mayflower Hotel in Washington, DC, on the need for an international Christian graduate university. The theologian did not hold back on the subject. His recollections provide a window into how he viewed the frustration of the formation of a research institution: "For $10 apiece we could have done it—there are over 30 million adult evangelicals in the United States. But we didn't and we have paid a high price."

In terms resonant with Harold Ockenga's 1947 Fuller address, Henry argued that America had suffered spiritually as a result of the church's inability to effectively answer secular challenges: "Secular humanism continues to snipe at the supernatural, to undermine God's revealed truth and his moral commands. We have good evangelical colleges, even some universities in the making, but we haven't fully fazed modern secular culture with the Christian worldview." He closed with a peroration showing that his zeal for his grand plan had not waned:

> Let there be scientists who behold God's glory and nature and not only impersonal processes; anthropologists who affirm the image of God is man and not only an animal ancestry; philosophers who stress that fear of God is the beginning of wisdom rather than the beginning of mythology; moralists who emphasize God's commandments rather than the tolerances of modern culture; artists who set *agape* to music and poetry and who will capture our now wicked world of words for whatever is good and godly; let us have intellectual leaders who offer life and hope to civilization that has missed the way and needs to be alerted again to the incomparable greatness and grace of Jesus Christ.[57]

Three decades after his initial conversations with Graham, the potential of a school still captivated Henry, as his comments show. The ideal graduate schools envisioned by Henry had shifted (as they had in previous communiqués), this time to "theology, medicine, history, philosophy of science, literature and the arts." The failure to found such a school by evangelicals rankled Henry; he believed that the movement had "paid a high price" as a result. As he saw it, the school could have provided a counter to "secular humanism," filled as it would have been with scholars grounded in the rich theological resources of Christianity yet engaging on the front lines with secular academicians. Henry surely admired many scholarly peers who worked with similar burdens, but he believed that a university could have enhanced and magnified such scholarship for the greater good of Christianity and the country more generally.

Frustrated as he was over the course of his career, the scholar never did finally give up on his hopes for an elite Christian university. In a letter to Craig Tavani in April 1988, he discussed with excitement the prospect of a new evangelical college. Writing in preparation for a trip to Oxford, Henry noted that he was ostensibly going to give a paper and listen to others. Instead, he confessed, "the hidden agenda of the Oxford conference's discussion of the possibility of launching CS Lewis College on the edge of a major secular university in the US—either West Coast, Midwest or East Coast."[58] The idea had some promise. Little concrete action ensued, though. One year later, Henry wrote to T. Grady Spires of Gordon College, another attendee, to inquire further. "Anything new about CS Lewis College?" he wrote, noting that he had heard nothing further."[59] Despite this lack of momentum, he continued to champion the college into the twilight years of his career, though it never materialized.

The preceding body of material reveals in fresh detail the great ambitions of the neo-evangelicals in general and the Cambridge evangelicals in particular. Like Ockenga, who personally befriended many of the future leaders, Henry cast a bold vision for a Christian research university. To his peers, big-money businessmen, beguiled *Christianity Today* readers, conferences of academics, and many more, Henry spun his vision of a grand institution founded on the kind of worldview thinking that drove Fuller Seminary and other postwar evangelical ventures. It is not too much to say that the elite Christian university was the prevailing hope—if not occupation—of Henry's adult life.

He worked on many projects, publishing more than thirty books, including the landmark six-volume work *God, Revelation, and Authority,* held professorships of one kind or another at multiple evangelical schools, and lectured all over the world. On a level reached by no other evangelical except for Graham and Ockenga, Henry was an evangelical statesman. His life was ferociously busy, and it would be a misnomer to suggest that the formation of a great academy consumed him. But the idea inspired Henry for most of his life and never sat far from his thoughts, regardless of what discouragement he had recently faced.

Fellow Cambridge evangelical Kenneth Kantzer offered such a perspective when he reflected in *Christianity Today* on Henry's career in 1993. Kantzer reported that "[f]rom his student days, Carl dreamed of a great Christian university modeled after sixteenth-century Wittenberg or Geneva."[60] Kantzer offered a cautious assessment of the great plan: "Perhaps the idea was ill-advised. Augustine taught us a millennium-and-a-half ago that Christianity is best understood not high in an ivory tower, but in the roaring thoroughfares of real life. In the radical pluralism of the modern world, a thousand rays of light may penetrate better than a single beam from a lighthouse."[61] The point is worth considering, as is the way the pursuit of a university by Henry and others sheds light on the paradoxical nature of the neo-evangelical movement.

The neo-evangelicals possessed an impressive ability to transcend past differences, to get a wide range of Christians at the table, and to work very hard for the promotion of worthy causes. They showed such skills in plotting the elite school many of them desired. Yet the same qualities that brought them together could also hinder their efforts. Their associations were not binding. They struggled in places to find common doctrinal and, in the case of Crusade University, moral ground. The plethora of existing institutions that the statesman-entrepreneurs created—a major sign of movement vitality—also made it difficult to squeeze in the one project that might have become a truly formidable institution.

The reasons why the school was never established are varied and complex. It is clear from the preceding material (and previous chapters) that the neo-evangelicals thought in big terms from robust theology and a cooperative stance. Sometimes they attempted great things and succeeded, as in the formation of Fuller; other times they pursued ambitious ends and failed, as in the case of Crusade University. It is not only in the projects that succeeded that we see the capacious intellectual ambitions of Henry and his fellow neo-evangelicals. Their failures—specifically, their inability to found Crusade University despite much plotting and planning—show us just how big the vision was, how grand the hopes were, and how fragile the evangelical movement proved to be.

CONCLUSION

The Intellectual Successes, Failures, and Fresh Prospects of Evangelicalism

In 1976, Harold Ockenga wrote the foreword to Harold Lindsell's *Battle for the Bible* from the steep-banked hills of Gordon-Conwell Theological Seminary. This was a moment late in Ockenga's life that paralleled an earlier one. Nearly fifty years before, he wrote to his girlfriend from Pasadena, telling her excitedly of a new seminary that he would soon attend. When Ockenga wrote from Pasadena, his location represented his future. When he wrote in South Hamilton, Massachusetts, his location represented his break with the past. The heady days at Fuller were over. Gordon-Conwell represented the second iteration of his dream for a transdenominational seminary grounded in conservative evangelical conviction.

In 1976, Ockenga expressed concern over the future of evangelicalism: "As evangelicalism grows, it becomes more and more threatened with incipient division. The perplexing question of the inspiration of Scripture is endangering the unity of the evangelical movement." For this reason, Ockenga avowed that "[t]he time has come to warn evangelicals of the incipient danger to both faith and practice which comes from abandoning the essentially orthodox view of Scripture."[1] It was not always thus. Much had transpired in the decades since Ockenga and the Cambridge evangelicals launched their ambitious thought-project. The young scholars Ockenga mentored and interacted with during their student days in Boston had gone on, most of them, to have impressive careers as evangelical leaders and academics. A real movement had developed in the 1940s, one that Ockenga steered and promoted to great effect.

In what follows, we trace the fruition of this movement, considering the postwar contributions of the graduate students Ockenga marshaled as the officer corps of intellectual neo-evangelicalism. This survey shows that the Cambridge evangelicals made good on their promise, as Ockenga himself did. This leads to a final reflection with four specific considerations on the significance of intellectual neo-evangelicalism for modern evangelicalism.

Edward John Carnell, brightest of the Cambridge evangelicals, became the second president of Fuller Theological Seminary in 1954. Carnell had fulfilled his early promise as a scholar of theology and philosophy, publishing *An Introduction to Christian Apologetics* in 1948, a prescient work titled *Television: Servant or Master?* in 1950, *The Theology of Reinhold Niebuhr* in 1950, and *A Philosophy of the Christian Religion* in 1952. With many others, Carnell believed that Ockenga was the best man for the job. But Ockenga never came west. This left an on-campus leadership vacuum that Carnell was tapped to fill.

It was a poor match from the start. Carnell was brilliant, but the challenges of fundraising, public relations, and administration strained Carnell from the moment he took the job. He was a scholar, not a president. Though Ockenga and others attempted to increase major donor contributions to the school, Fuller struggled during Carnell's tenure to raise adequate funds and endowment. Over time, this took a toll on his health. Alongside numerous writing projects and a demanding schedule of speaking and teaching, these factors conspired to force Carnell to resign the presidency at the end of the 1958–59 year.

In the years that followed, Ockenga warmly encouraged his protégé to continue writing. This Carnell did even as he fought for health. In the midst of Carnell's trials, Ockenga told him that he longed "to see come from your pen a whole series of books on a great theological doctrine—something like Berkouwer has done or something from the evangelical point of view like Nels Ferre [*sic*] has done from the liberal point of view." In Ockenga's estimation, "Nobody is better equipped to do this than yourself, and the evangelical world is crying out for the kind of literature which you can write."[2]

Carnell published *Christian Commitment: An Apologetic* with MacMillan in 1957, *The Case for Orthodox Theology* with Westminster Press in 1959, and *The Kingdom of Love and the Pride of Life* with Eerdmans in 1960. He found himself in a different place in the final years of his life, however. "Sometimes," he confided to Ockenga, "anxiety rolls over me with the force of a terrible tidal wave." Nonetheless, he soldiered on, telling Ockenga in July 1961 that he was "working on a manuscript, *The Gentle Art of Christian Witnessing*, but I not sure [*sic*] anything will come of it." His family had gone on vacation, leaving him with "the dog, my book, my bottle of sleeping pills, and the depressing realization that I am now deep into my second year as a psychiatric patient."[3]

Ockenga did not cease to encourage his friend. In February 1962, he wrote, saying, "I just want you to know, Ed, old boy, that we all love you and we desperately need you at the seminary so we are anxious to have you take plenty of time off and fully recover." Carnell thanked him for this and other missives, remembering fondly as he did so his days when he was "a student at Harvard and a member of Park Street Church." In one of the final letters from Ockenga to Carnell, the pastor warmly recounted their past times of fellowship, remembering "those times when you and I and Leonard used to go to the radio station to discuss some subject. I certainly wish you were closer at hand and we could have times of fellowship together."[4]

It was not to be. Carnell died in 1967 in mysterious circumstances, his final years difficult. His death does not seem to be occasioned by his commitment to inerrancy or conservative theology, but was likely the result of overwork and overweening vocational anxiety.[5] Though Carnell did not single-handedly reposition the academic stature of evangelical philosophical theology—an impossible task—he nonetheless made major contributions to the guild.[6] By engaging with such figures as Soren Kierkegaard and Reinhold Niebuhr, Carnell demonstrated that evangelicals were fully capable of philosophical and theological engagement at the highest levels. Before his life and career were cut short, Carnell employed a fresh mode of cultural approach that married contextual awareness with theological analysis. His book *Television: Master or Servant?* foreshadowed the "cultural engagement" method of later evangelicals.

Kenneth Kantzer was not nearly as prolific a writer as Carnell, but he was better suited to the tasks of administration he took on at Trinity Evangelical Divinity School (TEDS). In 1962, Kantzer came to Trinity to serve as its founding dean. Kantzer found barely forty students waiting for him when he assumed his post. Though he intended to write monographs on Calvin and Barthian theology, Kantzer set aside various writing projects to lead the divinity school and draw an accomplished faculty.[7] His labors paid off. Three decades after he began his work, the student body numbered sixteen hundred and the faculty had established itself as one of the finest in the evangelical world, if not the finest.[8] Eminent scholars like Harold O. J. Brown, David Wells, D. A. Carson, John Woodbridge, George Marsden, and Carl F. H. Henry served at Trinity during Kantzer's tenure and made significant contributions to evangelical theology even as they helped to establish evangelicals as a legitimate scholarly presence in exegetical, historical, theological, philosophical, and missiological disciplines.

It took great effort to fund and build such a school. At TEDS,

Kantzer faced the financial burdens that tax the energies of many a school administrator. To keep the divinity school and college running at full steam, Kantzer assumed numerous positions over the course of his career, including a stint as president of the college from 1982 to 1983. During the 1970s and '80s, Kantzer held major leadership positions at *Christianity Today.* He served the magazine as editor-in-chief from 1978 to 1982, leaving the divinity school during this period.[9] His passion, however, was TEDS, where he emphasized a strong commitment to theological education driven by a passion for Jesus Christ and rigorous Christian scholarship of such a high standard that it would require consideration on the part of the broader academy.[10]

Samuel Schultz and Meryl Tenney each taught at Wheaton College. From 1949 to 1980, Schultz taught Old Testament; he served for many years as the chair of the Department of Biblical Studies. He wrote *The Old Testament Speaks,* a textbook translated into twenty languages and reprinted in numerous editions. Tenney served as dean of the Wheaton College Graduate School from 1947 to 1971. He came to Wheaton from Gordon College. During the course of his career, he wrote numerous commentaries and books on the New Testament, including *New Testament Times, The Vital Heart of Christianity,* and *Galatians, the Charter of Christian Liberty.*

John H. Gerstner taught Church History at Pittsburgh Theological Seminary for more than thirty years, establishing himself as an evangelical authority on Jonathan Edwards. His major contribution was a three-volume set titled *The Rational Biblical Theology of Jonathan Edwards.* D. G. Hart has suggested that "[b]efore John H. Gerstner wrote *Steps to Salvation: The Evangelistic Message of Jonathan Edwards* (1959), the production of books on Edwards averaged numbers in the low single digits throughout the 1950s." In successive decades, academic interest in Edwards exploded, thanks in large part to the Jonathan Edwards Center at Yale University and the efforts of evangelical scholars like Gerstner. The historian did not publish many books, but he established himself as an evangelical academic of repute.

Two of the Cambridge evangelicals worked for many years at Gordon College. Burton Goddard held numerous positions at Gordon College and Divinity School, including Dean and Director of the library. He served as the first general secretary and as an editor and translator of the Committee on Bible Translation, which in 1978 produced the New International Version of the Bible. Roger Nicole taught theology at the seminary for forty-one years. Nicole served as president of the Evangelical Theological Society and was a founding member. He was also a founding member of the International Council on Biblical Inerrancy.

Nicole did not author many texts, but his contributions to systematic theology on specific subjects were profound. His role as a mentor to students, including future evangelical leaders like Mark Dever, pastor of Capitol Hill Baptist Church, was also significant. Dever later remembered that "Roger Nicole modeled exacting scholarship and at the same time a generosity of spirit toward those with whom he disagreed. His defenses of inerrancy and definite atonement, his preference for being addressed as 'brother', his kindness to children and joy in living, all encouraged and instructed me."[11]

One who worked closely with many at Gordon was Terrelle Crum, dean for many years of the Providence Bible Institute in Rhode Island. Until it became part of Barrington College, the school was one of only two Christian liberal arts institutions in New England. One of Crum's colleagues at the Boston School of the Bible was Gleason Archer. In 1948, Ockenga drew Archer from Park Street to Fuller, where he served as Professor of Biblical Languages until 1965. Archer left Fuller in 1965 to become professor of Old Testament at Trinity. Archer became well-known for his *Encyclopedia of Bible Difficulties*, which went through many printings, as well as his stance on inerrancy.

Paul King Jewett taught systematic theology at Fuller for three decades. Like many of his fellow Boston scholars, Jewett was a Baptist and wrote a text on baptism that became the standard articulation of the credo-Baptist position, titled *Infant Baptism and the Covenant of Grace.* Like Nicole, Jewett advocated egalitarian convictions on gender roles, publishing such influential works as *Man as Male and Female.* Glen Barker served with Jewett at Fuller and became the school's first Provost. One of Fuller's first administrators, Harold Lindsell, sparked one of the major Christian controversies of the twentieth century when he published *The Battle for the Bible* in 1976. The book, carrying a foreword from Ockenga, answered ongoing theological drift in a fearless style. Like Henry and Kantzer, Lindsell served as editor of *Christianity Today* for several years. Lindsell wrote prolifically and taught law following his retirement from the magazine.

The scholarship of George Eldon Ladd ranked second to none among his evangelical peers of the postwar twentieth century, with texts like *The Gospel of the Kingdom, A Theology of the New Testament,* and *The Presence of the Future* representing some of the most significant New Testament monographs of the twentieth century. As John D'Elia has shown, Ladd's writings in the field of New Testament set the context for discussions of kingdom and eschatology for decades to come.[12] Like Carnell, Ladd invested his body and soul in the project of lending academic credibility to evangelical scholarship in his field. Unfortunately, this investment cost Ladd a great deal, eroding his ties to his family. Nevertheless, as D'Elia has concluded, "generations of highly regarded evangelical scholars owe an unpaid debt to George Ladd for opening doors to them at the highest levels of academic discourse, and making possible their place at the table."[13]

The leader of these and other members of the Cambridge evangelicals was Harold John Ockenga. After leaving Fuller and completing his ministry at Park Street Church in 1969, Ockenga served as the founding president of Gordon-Conwell Theological Seminary (GCTS). GCTS opened its doors in 1970. The seminary opened with 286 students in 1969; by the time of his retirement in 1978, it enrolled 641 students. The most significant mark Ockenga left on the school was grounded in his lectures and chapel messages; the school continues an annual lectureship in preaching named for Ockenga.[14] The president continued the breathless pace of his ministry even in his later years, traveling widely in an ongoing effort to offer leadership and guidance to the next generation of evangelical luminaries. This did not prevent Ockenga from building an esteemed faculty that included such scholars as David Wells, Nicole, and Garth Rosell.

Ockenga's ministry exercised a dramatic effect on a number of future evangelical leaders. Two of the most prominent are pastor John Piper and theologian Wayne Grudem. John Piper, Chancellor of Bethlehem College and Seminary, was a student at Wheaton College in the fall of 1966 when Ockenga came to campus to preach in Chapel. Piper did not attend chapel but nonetheless felt his heart stirred by Ockenga's preaching, as he later recounted: "I was lying in the campus health center with mono [mononucleosis] as I listened to him on the radio. And God created in my heart at that time a desire to study and understand and teach the Word of God that has never died. It is as alive and strong today as it ever was."[15] Piper went on to study at Fuller, where Daniel Fuller influenced his theology, moving on to the University of Munich for his PhD. He later taught at Bethel Seminary in St. Paul, Minnesota, before becoming pastor of Bethlehem Baptist Church in Minneapolis.[16] Piper's preaching and writing helped to spark what some have called the "young, restless, and reformed" movement among a wide swath of Christian youth.[17]

Wayne Grudem, Research Professor of Theology and Biblical Studies at Phoenix Seminary, has worked toward similar ends throughout his career as a theologian. He began his career, like Piper, due to his encounter with the searching preaching of the Park Street pastor while a Harvard undergraduate. Grudem reflected on this calling in an interview: "I attended Park Street Church and sat under Ockenga's teaching from the late fall of 1967 (my freshman year) until my graduation from Harvard in June, 1970. I had gone to Harvard with the goal of attending law school after college and then entering politics."

It was Ockenga's preaching that changed the course of his life, however. "As I listened to Harold Ockenga's detailed expository preaching both Sunday morning and Sunday evening (I never wanted to miss Sunday evening's sermon!), God worked in my heart to persuade me to go to seminary and enter full-time ministry rather than pursue law and politics."[18] During his training at Harvard, Grudem found Ockenga's preaching a singularly captivating experience. Even at the close of his career, Ockenga made a strong impression on brilliant young students. Grudem later studied at Cambridge University for his doctorate in New Testament. He taught at Bethel Seminary before joining the faculty of Trinity Evangelical Divinity School, where he authored a highly influential systematic theology textbook that has sold hundreds of thousands of copies.[19]

Piper and Grudem represent a tiny sample of those involved in intellectually driven Christian ministry whom Ockenga influenced. They are but two of the most influential evangelicals of the twenty-first century who trace their commitment to ministry, one emphasizing both the mind and the heart, directly to him. This owed not only to Ockenga's unusual gifts but also to his strategic vision and his spiritual ambition. He was the indispensable man of neo-evangelicalism, the one without whom no major enterprise could be projected. Under his leadership, the Cambridge evangelicals sought, in Carnell's arresting phrase, a "thorough shakedown" of the Christian intellect. Without Ockenga, there would have been no such attempt.

Long after Carnell penned that memorable phrase, the neo-evangelicals recognized in their twilight years that they had accomplished something unusual. Roger Nicole, a member of the Cambridge evangelicals, contributed an article to *Christianity Today* in 1996 that sketched the outcome of the movement in question. He pointed out that "[i]n 1945, only a handful of seminaries that were accredited members of the American Association of Theological Schools could clearly rate as evangelical. In 1995, there were 125 accredited Protestant seminaries in the United States." Nicole went on to suggest that evangelical scholarly literature had experienced a Gutenberg-like explosion following the 1940s. "In 1945, a common complaint was that evangelicals were not producing works of scholarship in biblical, historical, and theological disciplines, let alone philosophy, psychology, sociology, and other fields less closely related to the seminary curriculum. Some of our greatest scholars—B. B. Warfield, J. Gresham Machen, and Abraham Kuyper—had died." In this day, "Evangelicals were chided for relying on book reprints, and the great publishing companies (Scribners, Harper's, Macmillan, and Oxford) turned their backs on evangelical production."

Fifty years later, Nicole argued that the state of evangelical scholarship was altogether changed. "By 1995, there were evangelical introductions to and biblical theologies of the Old and New Testaments, not to speak of numerous monographs in biblical archaeology, history, hermeneutics, and linguistics." Beyond biblical studies and theology, "Evangelicals have produced works on history, psychology, pastoral theology, homiletics, family relations, the devotional life, denominational distinctive, and scores of other subjects." What once was a curiosity had become an industry, according to Nicole: "The problem in 1945 was that we had relatively few new conservative books; the problem now is that there are so many that few people can afford to purchase all those they would like to own."[20]

This strength of program extended to the proliferation of libraries at evangelical seminaries. When Fuller Seminary began in 1947, Ockenga boasted of its collection of around twenty-five thousand books. In 1995, Nicole tabulated that "at least 25 evangelical seminaries have libraries exceeding 100,000 volumes, the largest being Calvin Theological Seminary with 478,000 volumes. Gordon-Conwell now has over 150,000 volumes, a growth of 3,000 percent since 1945."[21] The picture was clear. These and other data showed great "gains of evangelicals in the United States since 1945." The seminary statistics available to Nicole in 1995, with "44 percent of the total" enrollment of all schools centering in "clearly evangelical" institutions, suggested to the Cambridge evangelical the realization of "a spectacular shift in the center of gravity of theological education in this country."[22]

The foregoing suggests that the neo-evangelicals themselves believed that a genuine disruption of anti-scholarly evangelicalism had occurred in the 1940s and following. Their conclusions accord with the narrative and thesis argued in these pages. This is not to oversell the neo-evangelicals. They did not succeed in all their aims, to be sure. They could be overconfident. They had a fairly large chip on their shoulder, and they were not always aware of their ambitious temperament. Many were from humble, working-class origins, and they embodied not only a high-minded scholarly bent but an inability to slow down in their work. They had a movement to acquit, after all, and they were determined to accomplish this feat in one generation. Under such self-imposed pressure and a real desire to dig conservative Protestants out of their cultural burial ground, they showed at times a propensity to high-strung behavior. They did not produce scholarly literature or educational institutions that vanquished secularism. They frequently critiqued fundamentalism for its failure to engage the culture at large, but they showed greater ability in creating new evangelical institutions than in crashing the lecture halls of the great secular universities.

This should not obscure the striking effects wrought by Ockenga and his young scholarly friends, though. There is a golden chain that runs through the various contours of this monograph. In Ockenga's formal education, his preaching at the intellectually demanding Park Street Church, the Boston School of the Bible, the Plymouth Scholars' Conferences, Fuller Theological Seminary, Henry's *Uneasy Conscience*, Graham's intellectual vision for *Christianity Today*, the Evangelical Theological Society, and Crusade University, we see the enfleshment of an intellectual project that inspired and catalyzed many in its day. Ties to these works are many and varied, but the vigorous evangelical intellectualism of the present day surely owes much to the legacy, however hidden it may be, of the neo-evangelicals.

Prodded and cultivated by Ockenga, the Cambridge evangelicals (and peers not mentioned here) published widely, established and contributed to academic societies and journals, worked in administration in newly formed seminaries and colleges, encouraged one another in scholarship, and even sought to found the great Christian research university, the school that encapsulated the soaring cultural and intellectual ambitions of the Cambridge evangelicals and many of their peers. Though Crusade faltered, many less Promethean efforts flourished. In a day when many fundamentalists and conservative Protestants had given up on such lofty aims, Ockenga, Henry, Graham, Carnell, and others dared to think, strategize, fundraise, and tirelessly promote the idea of a new intellectual program.

The project led by Ockenga and championed by Graham, Henry, and others was so connected, so sprawling, that it undoubtedly left a mark on many who might not even know of it. The Cambridge evangelicals grew up with Billy Sunday disavowing theology entirely and John R. Rice warning his readership of the dangers of "scholarship." Just a few years later, Ockenga convened oceanside gatherings of Christian scholars who gave voice to a common desire to address the ill fortunes of the evangelical mind. Five decades hence, this vision was enacted by dozens of Christian intellectuals who were, in Alan Wolfe's estimation, "writing the books, publishing the journals, teaching the students, and sustaining the networks necessary to establish a presence in American academic life."[23]

Richard Mouw, then president of Fuller Theological Seminary and a widely respected theologian, concurred in his assessment of contemporary evangelical academic life. "Today there is a greater appreciation for the intellectual life. Evangelical colleges and seminaries are more inclined these days to support good scholarship on the grounds that thinking clearly about things is a healthy activity for the Christian community." Mouw cited The Council of Christian Colleges and Universities (CCCU) as a key factor in the development of this inclination. But this was not the only contributor: "[A] marvelous informal network of evangelical scholars" had sprung up that included many professors at "major secular universities." This included, according to Mouw, "Wolterstorff, Volf, and Stout at Yale; Plantinga, Marsden, and Hatch at Notre Dame; Wuthnow at Princeton; the outstanding faculties at Wheaton and Calvin."[24] This was but a partial list that includes many others.

Beyond the best-known professors, some researchers have uncovered a substantial evangelical professorial presence at secular colleges and universities. A 2009 study in the journal *Sociology of Religion* found that roughly 19 percent of a diverse group of college professors described themselves as "born-again Christian." Professors at four-year schools claiming this term represented 24.6 percent of all respondents.[25] The American academy is now as ever a place for evangelicals to ply their trade. Ockenga and the Cambridge evangelicals would have celebrated this reality, though they would also have noted that the same journal article concluded that only 1 percent of professors at elite universities claimed the "born again" label. In the Christian higher education community, schools continue to proliferate and expand. The CCCU, founded in 1975 with thirty-eight member institutions, boasts a twelve-million-dollar budget and by its own accounting serves 119 institutions in North America with fifty-five affiliate institutions in twenty countries.[26]

Evangelical academia is filled with schools seeking to expand their campuses, establish more cornerstone programs in general disciplines like the hard sciences, and raise the caliber of their student body. In recent years, schools like Union University, Baylor University, Houston Baptist University, California Baptist University, and Boyce College have experienced major growth. At the liberal arts level, The King's College in New York City and Gordon College have championed a fresh commitment to traditional college curricula. The neo-evangelical vision of Henry, Graham, Ockenga, and others has not died. It is alive.

The foregoing offers a solid counter to the presentation of the neo-evangelicals in some prominent historical work of the current day. Molly Worthen's *Apostles of Reason* has justly drawn attention for its richly resourced and literarily invigorating material. The overall portrait of the evangelical movement and its leaders in *Apostles of Reason* is not overly positive, however. "The cult of the Christian worldview" has, according to Worthen, "crippled evangelicals" in their effort to engage the culture.[27] Many would agree that the American church has suffered what Worthen calls a "crisis of authority," but it is not immediately clear that the genesis of this crisis is in worldview thinking, so-called, but in distrust of the Bible, particularly contested portions and doctrines of the Bible. The church's handling of sexual ethics in the last thirty years suggests that it does indeed struggle to affirm biblical authority when the culture presses in.

Worthen also reads expansive political motives into the neo-evangelical platform. As this monograph has shown, leading lights of evangelicalism did wish to recover a conservative political spirit in America. But Worthen stretches when she groups all efforts to think systemically as "soft presuppositionalism" in pursuit of a "viable political currency" that would allow Christians to "buy cultural capital." At times—and her tone alternately warms and cools throughout *Apostles of Reason*—Worthen seems to read neo-evangelicalism as a movement that launched a half-hearted intellectual project in order to speed along its true initiative: dominating America politically. If this is correct, Worthen interprets the neo-evangelicals in light of the Religious Right of the 1980s and following. The latter was far more politically inclined than the latter, however.

One can scarcely read the letters, sermons, and articles of these and other evangelical leaders and conclude that they were anything but genuinely invested in the development of the Christian mind. This cause consumed Henry, as we have seen. It led Billy Graham to start numerous projects, including *Christianity Today*, originally plotted to be something close to an academic journal that would lead to theological renewal. It catalyzed Ockenga to launch intellectually rigorous schools seeking academic reconstruction on *both coasts*. This is just a sampling of the fruits of intellectual neo-evangelicalism. The movement was an earnest one, and there was considerable commonality of purpose among many evangelical scholars and institution-builders in the mid twentieth century.

This shared project faltered because of a lack of confidence in biblical authority, not because biblical authority as a concept is unworkable and untenable in light of secularity. Biblical authority allows for much greater coherence in terms of morality, ethics, rational inquiry, scientific questing, and epistemological confidence than does secularism. One begins from a revealed source, albeit a contested one (what is not contested in our world?); the other begins from a blank slate but asks all to assent to its blankness. The choice is stark, and the biblical option is, it must be said, inextricably linked to faith. But secularism, and a secular epistemology, requires no less faith. It takes serious commitment to get something from nothing, to derive assurance from skepticism, to read ought in what is, and to arraign meaning from chaos.

I agree with Worthen that evangelicals have struggled to trust the authority of Scripture. But this is not because the Bible is unintelligible or because postmodern hermeneutics have revealed its incoherence. Christians have been sorely challenged by secularism and have not always responded from a posture of theistic confidence.

This lack of brio does not signal that there is no evangelical mind. There is one, and its lack of existence has been greatly exaggerated. The evangelical mind is not rigidly narrow. The evangelical mind has offered the world a Trinitarian framework, which paved the way for cultural unity in diversity, and an enchanted anthropology, which led to care for "exposed" infants and sacrificial medical attention in times of plague. The evangelical mind created medieval universities united in a common view of God's truth. The evangelical mind unleashed the Protestant Reformation, sparked widespread support of (relatively) free markets and property rights, and helped spur on untold economic flourishing in the West. The evangelical mind inspired countless scientists to conduct technical inquiries in botany, geology, physics, and biology. The evangelical mind led to philosophical treatises by geniuses like Augustine, Aquinas, Calvin, Pascal, Edwards, Reid, Lewis, and Plantinga. If the evangelical mind is not always appreciated, this simply cannot be because it does not exist. It does exist, and its contributions over two millennia are monumental.

We must also inquire of its future prospects. Evangelicals, like fundamentalists, have built up their own networks and institutions. Yet they still hunger for broader academic influence. In what follows, I want to suggest four insights reaped from the program of the Cambridge evangelicals that may be of use to their heirs in future days.

First, the neo-evangelicals remind modern Christians of the value of institutions. The projects that allowed neo-evangelicalism to take wing idled until leaders like Ockenga, Graham, and Henry instantiated them in institutional form. Their lives grew more complex and busy because of this; essentially all of the Cambridge scholars paid a price, even a heavy one, for their institutional investments. But in creating schools and media outlets and conferences, this group ensured that its vision could not be easily dismissed. Many of the ventures of the neo-evangelicals live on nearly a century after their founding. This is no small accomplishment.[28]

Today, Christians should recognize afresh the capacity and potential of institutions. This is particularly true of academic institutions. A multi-tiered approach to the instantiation of ideas is preferable. Too often, evangelicals seek the "New Harvard" or nothing. It might serve the movement better in the long term to accept that different undertakings can serve different purposes. There is room, in other words, for a plethora of ventures, some grand, some midsized, some smaller.

There is a place for the small Christian college. It is not uncommon that such schools feel pressure to upgrade themselves. But this is a mistake, even a big one. The significance of the small college is well-established in the broader academy. Colleges like Williams, Middlebury, and Davidson enjoy excellent academic reputations. They offer undergraduates enhanced learning in comparison to much larger schools that must by definition stage many classes on an outsized scale. There is real but often under-valued gain in smaller classes, professorial attention to papers, and exchange of ideas with peers.

It is understandable that many colleges would wish to be taken seriously in the way that "R1" institutions are, boasting as they often do gleaming laboratories, superstar faculty, and one graduate program after another. Yet historically, small American colleges have made major contributions to public life. So it may be in small Christian colleges that recommit themselves to providing a truly excellent education for students. Such schools can seize the opportunities before them to offer a rich, immersive academic experience. There is a place for the small Christian college, and it is a choice one.

There is also a need for midsized Christian universities that equip a broader array of students for a wider range of vocations. The evangelical movement will benefit from the proliferation of such schools. Christians are called to every field, and so it is right that universities train in specialized ways the next generation of engineers, doctors, entrepreneurs, and lawyers. There need not be tension between the Christian liberal arts college and the Christian university. Both are vital.

In similar fashion, evangelicalism needs intellectually vibrant seminary training. Seminaries must continue to serve their traditional functions: training pastors and missionaries and ministry workers. The Cambridge evangelicals underplayed the role of the local church in kingdom work. In some cases, they considered polity and ecclesiology to be of only glancing importance relative to the gospel and the doctrine of Scripture. Their primary doctrine-focused methodology helped spur an adoctrinal eclecticism in later generations that has, ironically, made cooperation difficult to sustain. It may in hindsight be better for modern Christians to agree on the cardinal doctrines, take secondary doctrines seriously, and cooperate from a more confessional framework that does not end up reducing non-primary matters to the status of "take it or leave it."

Beyond colleges and seminaries, many Christians still desire to build and sustain a major research university. Decades, even centuries after being evacuated from the Ivy League, Christians still feel a profound sense of loss. One after another, the great universities slipped their surly confessional bonds, only to grow many times greater and more powerful in secular hands than in days past. This poignancy is not without justification. To a considerable degree, it is the loss of the elite academic institutions of America that has turned the tide of American culture. Most every significant shift away from the Judeo-Christian worldview of the American past is connected to, if not directly credited to, the elite universities and colleges of this country. The sexual revolution in its various phases, the marginalization of religious groups in public life, unfortunate segmentation in the name of diversity—these and many other developments of late modernity have received hearty backing from our leading academic institutions.

Recognition of this reality can lead evangelicals to despair. What Christians have lost they will likely never regain. Further, building schools of similar influence will prove difficult in the extreme. Such initiatives require big vision, unearthly capital, and buy-in from thousands of people, whether a receptive student body, faculty, administrators, and trustees. This is no small matter. But here we come to our second insight.

Second, the neo-evangelical experience speaks to the importance—but also the limitations—of grand strategy. With all the caveats stated, evangelicals should still seek to build great institutions. The neo-evangelicals created strong schools, many of which are still standing (though some are weathering the perils of theological compromise). They united in common cause. They wrote valuable books that have inspired future generations of scholars and leaders and public intellectuals. They re-engaged the culture, creating a prophetic ethical and philosophical witness. Perhaps we can sum up their accomplishments with a hypothetical: given a choice between a return to the evangelical circles of the 1930s or those of the 1950s, which would we prefer? The answer, for many Christians, is obvious.

In similar fashion, Christians who care about the life of the mind and who face the decision to invest in institutions and pursue the fulfillment of ambitious plans should not stand down. They should redouble their efforts. Our cultural moment in the early twenty-first century is remarkably similar to that which Ockenga and his fellow Cambridge evangelicals found themselves in during the 1930s. Today, evangelicals united by a common theological core should seek the construction of institutions that will strengthen the church's intellectual program, cultural interaction, and shared witness.

Third, the neo-evangelical legacy commends confessional scholarship. Many schools, including several championed and founded by the Cambridge scholars, have begun under the most auspicious of vision statements. "The evangelical Harvard" is, as noted, something of an academic grail, the mythic white whale that stalks the evangelical seas, never to be seized. The real challenge is more subtle. Can Christian colleges and universities not only tender outstanding instruction and establish themselves as centers of influence but also remain distinctively Christian? If believers are honest, there are very few schools that have safely navigated the Scylla of secularistic excellence and the Charybdis of internalized pietism.

The evangelical colleges and universities that are best positioned to take on such a mission are those that are confessional. They are grounded in a rich biblical-theological vision of the Christian life and witness, and most directly are anchored in a statement of faith that standardizes and norms teaching and scholarship. This is not to say that every department comprehensively formulates a distinctively scriptural form of its discipline—Christian dentistry, for example, as a unique calling in contradistinction to secular dentistry. It is to say that every department, every program, from top to bottom, views itself as powered by the biblical metanarrative. From roots to branches, every faculty member and administrator savors the reality of Christ crucified and risen. It is from this concept that models of vocation, classroom instruction, and institutional life spring.

This does not mean, of course, that every professor is a theologian—far from it. It does mean that among faculty members, individual commitment to Christ is essential. Christian scholars who teach with excellence and publish with top presses must nonetheless be more a Christian than they are a scholar. They must take care that they are more concerned to honor their God as a botanist or a historian or a biologist or an engineer or a journalist than they are to be famous, accomplished, and renowned in their field.

Some scholars may feel some resistance to such a seemingly humble profile. The broader academy, after all, rewards those who operate according to its dictates, damp down their convictions, and embrace secularist paradigms. Christian scholars will feel profound tension at times. The world and its promises will seem so desirous, and the kingdom of God will feel so small by comparison. But whether professors are located in non-Christian or Christian environments, they must take care to be Christians first, tethered to the Word of God without reservation, affirming the Bible as good.

Fourth, the neo-evangelicals commend the life of the mind to the modern church. The evangelical movement, as this book has shown, was affected in the early twentieth-century by what we could call spiritual pragmatism. Education was valued as that which imparted the basics of Christian belief and spirituality. The school served as a kind of religious technical college, training students to assume service in generally pragmatic fields: youth work, aviation, basic teaching, and the like. This mindset, which led to the creation of many biblically faithful Bible institutes and small Christian colleges, allowed for the preservation of the faith in the fractious early twentieth century. More than this, it enabled fundamentalists and conservative Christians to build their networks, send many missionaries to the field, and provide training for young believers that did not shipwreck their faith. All these are positive outcomes of prewar Christian education.

Regrettably, this model did not often inculcate in its students a zeal for the life of the mind. In fact, many Christian educators expressly avoided the intricacies of scholarship. In too many places, this avoidance was a badge of pride, a symbol of steadfast connection to a living faith that did not depend upon esoteric theological engagement for its sustenance. This outlook was understandable but also unfortunate. The divestment of involvement in the life of the mind meant, unsurprisingly, that the church had very little to say about the life of the mind. Onlookers could easily conclude that Christianity was only a practical religion, not an intellectual one.

This is a view that suffers from a host of deficiencies. According to Scripture, God himself created humankind. Man and woman bear his image (Gen. 1:26–27). Like God, the human person is a thinking being, and is conscious of this activity. In light of this teaching, the biblical worldview does not stultify the life of the mind. It unleashes it.

The neo-evangelicals saw that thinking is an irreducible good. They considered the intellect an instrument of pleasure, not mere utility. They understood that thinking is a matter of obedience to God. So says the First and Greatest Commandment: "love the Lord your God with all your heart, soul, and mind" (Matt. 22:37). The mind is according to Jesus Christ an instrument of love, and thus a means of worship. One could spend a lifetime plumbing the depths— and the heights—of this divine call. Scholars are those who have the chance to do so.

The same questions that confronted the neo-evangelicals greet modern Christians. Great gains have been made. Mark Noll once derided the "scandal" of the evangelical mind, noting that there was not much of one.[29] In more recent years, however, Noll has observed that "evangelical intellectual life is being strengthened" by numerous positive developments: academically serious Christian colleges, increased numbers of Christian scholars on secular campuses, and the ongoing vibrancy of confessional seminaries, among others.[30] It remains to be seen just how strong the movement, if such a sprawling collection of institutions and individuals may be called a movement, will become. Perhaps it has reached its apotheosis.

Perhaps not. Certainly, the neo-evangelical example might suggest otherwise. The young thinkers who identified serious intellectual problems in prewar fundamentalism ended up repositioning their movement along academic and intellectual lines. They did so in the face of the challenges of their own age. Despite evangelical acedia, a lack of vision, few precedents, and no formal program, Ockenga and the Cambridge evangelicals created Fuller Seminary, *Christianity Today*, a host of new colleges and universities, and a resurgent body of scholarly literature.

Successive generations of thinkers and leaders serving at faithful and rigorous institutions show that the evangelical mind cannot any more be described as a scandal. Many years ago, an ancient instinct revived among conservative American evangelicals. Modern Christians themselves are confronted with remarkably similar circumstances in a secularizing culture and an increasingly hostile public square. The church faces a profound choice: it can retreat and huddle, nursing its wounds as it accepts its intellectual marginalization. Or, it can learn once more from Ockenga, Henry, Graham, and the Cambridge evangelicals, and promote outstanding education that not only engages the questing heart but freshly awakens the evangelical mind.[31]

NOTES

When citing the names of frequently appearing collections of papers in the notes, the following shortened references have been used:

HENRY PAPERS	Henry Papers, Rolfing Library, Trinity Evangelical Divinity School, Deerfield, Illinois
KANTZER PAPERS	Kantzer Papers, Rolfing Library, Trinity Evangelical Divinity School, Deerfield, Illinois
OCKENGA PAPERS	Ockenga Papers, Gordon-Conwell Theological Seminary, South Hamilton, Massachusetts
PARK STREET CHURCH PAPERS	Park Street Church Papers, Congregational Library, Boston, Massachusetts
THE VAULT	The Vault, Park Street Church, Boston, Massachusetts

Introduction

1. Alvin Plantinga, "A Christian Life Partly Lived," in *Philosophers Who Believe: The Spiritual Journeys of Eleven Leading Thinkers*, ed. Kelly James Clark (Downers Grove, Ill.: IVP Academic, 1997), 64.

2. Ibid.

3. Ibid.

4. Alan Wolfe, "Opening of the Evangelical Mind," *Atlantic Monthly*, October 2000.

5. D. Michael Lindsay, *Faith in the Halls of Power: How Evangelicals Joined the American Elite* (New York: Oxford Univ. Press, 2007), 107.

6. Ibid., 113.

7. For more on these institutions, see Arthur Matthews, *Standing Up, Standing Together: The Emergence of the National Association of Evangelicals* (Carol Stream, Ill.: National Association of Evangelicals, 1992); George Marsden, *Reforming Fundamentalism: Fuller Seminary and the New Evangelicalism* (Grand Rapids: Eerdmans, 1987); and Stephen Board, "Moving the World with Magazines: A Survey of Evangelical Periodicals," in *American Evangelicals and the Mass Media*, ed. Quentin J. Schultze (Grand Rapids: Zondervan, 1990), 171–95.

8. See James Davison Hunter, *To Change the World: The Irony, Tragedy, and Possibility of Christianity in the Late Modern World* (New York: Oxford Univ. Press, 2010), esp. 32–78.

9. For preliminary background on this group, see Joel A. Carpenter, *Revive Us Again: The Reawakening of American Fundamentalism* (Oxford: Oxford Univ. Press, 1997); Mark A. Noll, *The Scandal of the Evangelical Mind* (Grand Rapids: Eerdmans, 1994); Michael S. Hamilton, "The Fundamentalist Harvard: Wheaton College and the Continuing Vitality of American Evangelicalism, 1919–1965" (PhD diss., University of Notre Dame, 1995); and the eminently helpful chapter 8, "Renewing the Mind," in Garth M. Rosell, *The Surprising Work of God: Harold John Ockenga, Billy Graham, and the Rebirth of Evangelicalism* (Grand Rapids: Baker, 2008), 187–212.

10. For more on the insecurities of the neo-evangelicals, see Molly Worthen, *Apostles of Reason: The Crisis of Authority in American Evangelicalism* (Oxford: Oxford Univ. Press, 2013). For research that sheds light on the different varieties of evangelicalism in the later stages of the movement, see David Swartz, *Moral Minority: The Evangelical Left in an Age of Conservatism* (Philadelphia: Univ. of Pennsylvania Press, 2012).

11. See Gregory A. Thornbury, *Recovering Classic Evangelicalism: Applying the Wisdom and Vision of Carl F. H. Henry* (Carol Stream, Ill.: Crossway, 2013). Keller has used the phrase in numerous talks and lectures. See, for example, his 2007 EMA lectures in London.

12. Noll, *Scandal of the Evangelical Mind*, 3.

Chapter 1: Boston Brahmin in Training

1. For more on J. Gresham Machen, see D. G. Hart, *Defending the Faith: J. Gresham Machen and the Crisis of Modern Protestantism in Modern America* (Phillipsburg, N.J.: P&R, 2003).

2. Harold J. Ockenga to Virginia Ray, July 27, 1929, Ockenga Papers.

3. Ibid., February 26, 1928.

4. Harold Lindsell, *Park Street Prophet: A Life of Harold John Ockenga* (Wheaton, Ill.: Van Kampen, 1951), 14.

5. Ibid., 14–22.

6. Harold J. Ockenga, "Who's Who" application, Ockenga Papers, The Vault.

7. John Adams, "The Making of a Neo-Evangelical Statesman: The Case of Harold John Ockenga" (PhD diss., Baylor University, 1994), 106.

8. Harold J. Ockenga, "Journal," April 23, 1927, Ockenga Papers.

9. Ibid. He did a considerable caveat to the effect that he could "see nothing really wrong with good drama if it is acted by good people."

10. Lindsell, *Park Street Prophet*, 23.

11. Garth M. Rosell notes that Ockenga preached more than four hundred times during college. See *The Surprising Work of God: Harold John Ockenga, Billy Graham, and the Rebirth of Evangelicalism* (Grand Rapids: Baker, 2008), 46.

12. "A Preacher That Will Attract," *New York Times*, October 6, 1884, 8.

13. Stan Gundry, personal correspondence, March 15, 2014.

14. Garth M. Rosell notes that the seven-year-long correspondence between Ockenga and Ray serves as an "amazing window" into the preacher's early life. Rosell, *Surprising Work*, 50.

15. Harold J. Ockenga to Virginia Ray, December 17, 1926, Ockenga Papers.

16. For more on Sunday and the youth culture of the early to mid-twentieth century, see Roger A. Bruns, *Preacher: Billy Sunday and Big-Time American Evangelism* (Urbana, Ill.: Univ. of Illinois, 1992), 48–61.

17. Harold J. Ockenga to Virginia Ray, April 26, 1927, Ockenga Papers.

18. Ockenga, "Journal," January 18, 1928.

19. For more on charismatic theology and Keswick influence, see Grant Wacker, *Heaven Below: Early Pentecostals and American Culture* (Cambridge: Harvard Univ. Press, 2001), 2–4; Vinson Synan, *Holiness-Pentecostal Tradition* (Grand Rapids: Eerdmans, 1997), 22–43; Andrew David Naselli, *Let Go and Let God: A Survey and Analysis of Keswick Theology* (Seattle: Logos, 2010), chaps. 2–3.

20. Ockenga, "Journal," May 23, 1927.

21. Ibid., June 18, 1926.

22. Harold J. Ockenga to Virginia Ray, July 20, 1927, Ockenga Papers.

23. Ibid., September 26, 1927.

24. Ibid., October 5, 1927.

25. Ockenga, "Journal," January 18, 1928.

26. Harold J. Ockenga to Virginia Ray, November 15, 1927, Ockenga Papers.

27. Harold J. Ockenga, "Middler Preaching Notes for Dr. J. R. Smith, Prof. First Term, 1928–29," November 1, 1928, Ockenga Papers.

28. Ibid., comments from "Mr. Wheeler."

29. Ibid., comments from "Dr. Smith."

30. The prize was the Robert L. Maitland Prize in New Testament exegesis. See Rosell, *Surprising Work*, 55.

31. Ockenga, "Journal," April 12, 1928.

32. For more on this affair, see R. Todd Mangum, *The Dispensational-Covenantal Rift: The Fissuring of American Evangelical Theology from 1936–1944*, Studies in Evangelical History and Thought (Carlisle, Penn.: Paternoster, 2007), esp. 49–61. See also Bradley J. Longfield, *The Presbyterian Controversy: Fundamentalists, Modernists, and Moderates*, Religion in America (New York: Oxford Univ. Press, 1993), 28–53; J. Michael Utzinger, *Yet Saints Their Watch Are Keeping: Fundamentalists, Modernists, and the Development of Evangelical Ecclesiology, 1887–1937* (Macon, Ga.: Mercer Univ. Press, 2006), 239–68.

33. For more on the Toy controversy, see Gregory A. Wills, *The Southern Baptist Theological Seminary, 1859–2009* (New York: Oxford Univ. Press, 2009), 108–49; for more on the Briggs trial, see Mark S. Massa, "Mediating Modernism: Charles Briggs, Catholic Modernism, and an Ecumenical 'Plot,'" *Harvard Theological Review* 81, no. 4 (October 1988): 413–30.

34. See Fred G. Zaspel, *The Theology of B. B. Warfield: A Systematic Summary* (Carol Stream, Ill.: Crossway, 2010), 42–59; Paul C. Gutjahr, *Charles Hodge: Guardian of American Orthodoxy* (New York: Oxford Univ. Press, 2011), 345–86.

35. The five points were as follows: (1) belief in the inspiration of an inerrant Bible, (2) the virgin birth of Christ, (3) the belief in the death of Christ as an atonement for sin, (4) the bodily resurrection of Christ, (5) the historical reality of Christ's miracles. For more on the significance of the doctrinal deliverance, see George Marsden, *Fundamentalism and American Culture: The Shaping of Twentieth-Century Evangelicalism, 1870–1925* (1980; Oxford: Oxford Univ. Press, 2006), 117, 136–37, and Douglas A. Sweeney, *The American Evangelical Story: A History of the Movement* (Grand Rapids: Baker, 2005), 155–80.

36. Marsden, *Fundamentalism and American Culture*, 119.

37. For more on the historic nature of inerrancy, see John D. Woodbridge, "Evangelical Self-Identity and the Doctrine of Biblical Inerrancy," in *Understanding the Times: New Testament Studies in the Twenty-First Century; Essays in Honor of D. A. Carson on the Occasion of His Sixty-Fifth Birthday*, ed. Andreas J. Kostenberger and Robert W. Yarbrough (Carol Stream, Ill.: Crossway, 2011), 104–40.

38. Hart, *Defending the Faith*, 128.

39. Timothy George and John Woodbridge, *The Mark of Jesus: Loving in a Way the World Can See* (Chicago: Moody, 2005), 129. The discussion that follows on who exactly a fundamentalist is following Laws' avowal is profitable (130ff).

40. Sweeney, *American Evangelical Story*, 166.

41. Robert Miller Moat, *Harry Emerson Fosdick: Preacher, Pastor, Prophet* (New York: Oxford Univ. Press, 2005), 74–173.

42. Longfield, *Presbyterian Controversy*, 11–12.

43. J. Gresham Machen, *Christianity and Liberalism* (1923; repr., Grand Rapids: Eerdmans, 2009), 44–45.

44. Ibid., 43, 67.

45. Ibid., 6.

46. Marsden, *Fundamentalism*, 80–81.

47. Hart, *Defending the Faith*, 124–25.

48. Ibid., 126.

49. Ibid., 134–35.

50. Harold J. Ockenga to Virginia Ray, July 27, 1929, Ockenga Papers.

51. Rosell notes that Ockenga kept a file folder full of clippings about the controversy, indicating that he followed it closely. Rosell, *Surprising Work*, 59n109.

52. For more on Bowne, see Gary Dorrien, *The Making of American Liberal Theology: Imagining Progressive Religion, 1805–1900* (Louisville: Westminster John Knox, 2001), 371–92.

53. Harold J. Ockenga, "Book Review: The Principles of Ethics," Ockenga Papers.

54. In *The Church That Was Twice Born: A History of the First Presbyterian Church of Pittsburgh, Pennsylvania, 1773–1973* (Pittsburgh: Pickwick-Morcraft, 1973), Ernest Edwin Logan wrote that "[i]n 1930 the Reverend Harold J. Ockenga came to First Church as assistant to Dr. Macartney. The two men had much in common and worked well together. . . . Dr. Macartney, in spite of his stern outward appearance was an incorrigible

practical joker, and April first was always a red-letter day for him, especially if he had a new assistant. He had a habit of sending the youthful minister out to visit a Mr. and Mrs. Lyons in Highland Park. Eventually, after a fruitless hour the raw assistant would find that the only lions in Highland Park were in cages in the zoological gardens" (52).

55. J. Gresham Machen to Harold J. Ockenga, February 4, 1931, Ockenga Papers.

56. Harold J. Ockenga to J. Gresham Machen, February 9, 1933, Ockenga Papers.

57. J. Gresham Machen to Harold J. Ockenga, December 15, 1932, Ockenga Papers.

58. Edward Luttwak, "Franco-German Reconciliation: The Overlooked Role of the Moral Re-armament Movement," in *Religion: The Missing Dimension of Statecraft*, ed. Douglas Johnston and Cynthia Sampson (New York: Oxford Univ. Press, 1994), 37.

59. J. Gresham Machen to Harold J. Ockenga, May 11, 1933, Ockenga Papers.

60. Harold J. Ockenga to J. Gresham Machen, May 15, 1933, Ockenga Papers.

61. Harold J. Ockenga to Virginia Ray, September 3, 1930, Ockenga Papers.

62. Ibid.

63. "Legislators Weigh Fate of Pitt Gift," *Pittsburgh Press*, May 12, 1935. Apparently Gabbert became known as critical of religion: "I was given to understand," he said in official testimony given in a 1935 university-wide dispute about Pitt's approach to religion, "that there had been a considerable amount of criticism on the effect my classes had on the religion of students."

64. Harold J. Ockenga to Virginia Ray, October 11, 1932, Ockenga Papers.

65. See John Curran Hardin, "Retailing Religion: Business Promotionalism in American Christian Churches in the Twentieth Century" (PhD diss., University of Maryland, 2011).

66. Ibid., 8.

67. Ockenga published a total of twelve books in his life. Most were edited collections of his sermons. See Harold J. Ockenga, *These Religious Affections* (Grand Rapids: Zondervan, 1937); *Our Protestant Heritage* (Grand Rapids: Zondervan, 1938); *Have You Met These Women?* (Grand Rapids: Zondervan, 1940); *Every One That Believeth* (New York: Revell, 1942); *The Comfort of God* (New York: Revell, 1944); *The Spirit of the Living God* (New York: Revell, 1947); *Faithful in Christ Jesus* (New York: Revell, 1948); *The Church in God* (New York: Revell, 1956); *Protestant Preaching through Lent* (Grand Rapids: Eerdmans, 1957); *Power through Pentecost* (Grand Rapids:

Eerdmans, 1959); *The Epistles to the Thessalonians* (Grand Rapids: Baker, 1962); *Women Who Made Bible History* (Grand Rapids: Zondervan, 1962).

68. Over the course of his career, Ockenga earned seven honorary doctorates: Suffolk LittD. 1939; Bob Jones HumD, 1944; Houghton College LLD, 1946; Wheaton College DD, 1960; Norwich University LtD, 1962; Seattle Pacific College LitD, 1963; Fuller DD, 1963.

69. E. Brooks Holifield, *God's Ambassadors: A History of the Christian Clergy in America* (Grand Rapids: Eerdmans, 2007), 173.

70. Ibid., 245.

Chapter 2: "A Mighty Man of God"

1. Harold J. Ockenga to J. Gresham Machen, November 16, 1934, Ockenga Papers.

2. J. Gresham Machen to Harold J. Ockenga, November 19, 1934, Ockenga Papers.

3. A. Donald MacLeod, "A. Z. Conrad: Park Street Pioneer," *New England Reformed Journal* 16 (2000): 2. Like many of the figures bound up with the history of Park Street Church, Conrad deserves further historiographical attention. See Garth M. Rosell, *Boston's Historic Park Street Church: The Story of an Evangelical Landmark* (Grand Rapids: Kregel, 2009), 53–54; Margaret Lamberts Bendroth, *Fundamentalists in the City: Conflict and Division in Boston's Churches, 1885–1950* (Oxford: Oxford Univ. Press, 2005), 103–6.

4. A. Z. Conrad to George M. Watson, September 11, 1936, Park Street Church Papers.

5. To make Conrad's service possible, Withrow donated over 75 percent of his salary to Conrad.

6. A. Z. Conrad, ed., *Commemorative Exercises of the One Hundredth Anniversary of the Organization of Park Street Church* (Boston: Park Street Centennial Committee, 1909), 25.

7. Ibid.

8. H. Crosby Englizian, *Brimstone Corner: Park Street Church, Boston* (Chicago: Moody, 1968), 212.

9. Ibid., 213–14. For more on Sunday and early twentieth-century revivalism, see Lyle Dorsett, *Billy Sunday and the Redemption of Urban America* (Grand Rapids: Eerdmans, 1991). For an incisive look at the shape of American evangelicalism in this period, see George Marsden, *Fundamentalism and American Culture: The Shaping of Twentieth-Century Evangelicalism, 1870–1925* (1980; Oxford: Oxford Univ. Press, 2006).

10. Englizian, *Brimstone Corner*, 219. Margaret Lamberts Bendroth quotes Conrad as saying "I would rather preach than do anything else in the world." The prospect of hiring an assistant upset Conrad, leading him to refuse the idea for years. Bendroth, *Fundamentalists in the City*, 163–64.

11. Bendroth, *Fundamentalists in the City*, 164.

12. Englizian, *Brimstone Corner*, 221.

13. Ibid.

14. Ibid., 222–23. Conrad's congregation obviously found him a deeply insightful man. After sermons, Conrad would sometimes answer questions from the congregation. H. Crosby Englizian includes one sample set that shows the facility of the pastor's mind and the curiosity of the people: Are not the lipstick inebriates a serious menace today? What proportion of leisure should be spent for pleasure? If law controls, how can liberty be a fact? Why would it be an egregious blunder for the United States to recognize Russian Sovietism? Should not bank deposits be guaranteed? On what basis are delegates to the Republican Convention selected? Is not the present cost of coal unreasonable?

15. Ibid., 215.

16. J. Gresham Machen to Harold J. Ockenga, November 19, 1934, Ockenga Papers.

17. See Harold J. Ockenga to Virginia Ray, October 11, 1932, Ockenga Papers.

18. Garth M. Rosell, *The Surprising Work of God: Harold John Ockenga, Billy Graham, and the Rebirth of Evangelicalism* (Grand Rapids: Baker, 2008), 69–70.

19. See J. Gresham Machen to Harold J. Ockenga, November 19, 1934, Ockenga Papers.

20. Harold J. Ockenga to J. Gresham Machen, January 21, 1935, Ockenga Papers.

21. Rosell, *Surprising Work*, 74–75.

22. The church held its memorial service on January 31, 1937. The weekly bulletin expressed sadness at Conrad's death, but hope for the future: "One of the great words in Dr. Conrad's vocabulary was loyalty. He taught us to be loyal to Christ in every thought, word, and act of life. He taught us to be loyal to each other. He taught us to be loyal to the Church. Now is the time to show that virtue. Do not miss a service at the church. Bring strangers. Call on indifferent members. Pray that God will enable us to carry on and to inaugurate an even greater work for Him." Park Street Church, "Memorial Service for Dr. A. Z. Conrad," Park Street Church Bulletin, January 31, 1937, Park Street Church Papers.

23. "Historic Parish Home on 'Brimstone Corner,'" *Boston Herald,* Sunday May 18, 1941, The Vault. This article also notes that in January 1941, Ockenga received and turned down a unanimous call to become pastor of the First Presbyterian Church of Seattle. The massive church had nine thousand members and its own radio station. It was reputedly the largest of its kind and would have given Ockenga a considerably larger salary and pastoral footprint.

24. Harold J. Ockenga, "The Rebellion of Man against God's Sovereignty," Sermon 350, Ockenga Papers.

25. Harold J. Ockenga, "Athens Looks to Jerusalem," Sermon 1057, Ockenga Papers.

26. "Historic Parish Home," *Boston Herald.*

27. Harold J. Ockenga, "Jonathan Edwards and New England or the Apologetic of Protestantism," Sermon 589, Ockenga Papers.

28. Ibid., 17.

29. Harold J. Ockenga, "The Second Blessing, Sanctification and Holiness," sermon preached on February 4, 1940, at Park Street Church, Ockenga Papers.

30. Edward Charles White, *The Beauty of Holiness: Phoebe Palmer as Theologian, Revivalist, Feminist, and Humanitarian* (Grand Rapids: Zondervan/Francis Asbury, 1986), 27–66.

31. Harold J. Ockenga, "God Save America," sermon preached on September 10, 1939, at Park Street Church, Ockenga Papers.

32. Ockenga was an ardent nationalist and became more so with time. Gordon Hugenberger, interview by author, December 21, 2010, Park Street Church, Boston. This view was corroborated by David Howard Adeney, interview by Paul Ericksen, November 14, 1988, Wheaton College Archives, Wheaton, Illinois. Adeney spoke anecdotally of this matter: "I think the only time that Harold J. Ockenga made me feel a little bit uncomfortable [pauses] was... [laughs] when we were... The new lodge at Ceder Campus was being opened, and I had just started the missionary training camp there and we had quite a number of internationals there, and in his talk, Harold J. Ockenga talked about the greatest... the great important... importance of missions and their influence in... spreading American influence, and the value of... of missions related to American culture, and... the... America's position in the world, and I was rather uncomfortable with... with those remarks because of the international students who were with us at that time."

33. For more on Ockenga's involvement with the NAE, see Rosell, *Surprising*

Work, 161–86; Harold Lindsell, *Park Street Prophet: A Life of Harold John Ockenga* (Wheaton, Ill.: Van Kampen, 1951), 109–26. Though Ockenga was first president of the organization from 1942 to 1944 and served in numerous capacities with it, helping to make it the premier organizing entity for postwar evangelicals, this book does not concentrate on the pastor's association with it. The preceding texts each treat the role Ockenga played in the NAE, a role that focused less on intellectual matters than other endeavors of the pastor.

34. Harold J. Ockenga, "The Christian Faces Segregation and Other Social Problems," sermon preached in 1957, Ockenga Papers, 20.

35. The story sent a shockwave through the South and beyond. See, for example, "Pastor Says North Also Has Problem," *Columbus (Ga.) Ledger*, 8; "Minister Cites North's Deficiencies of Integration," *California Daily Enterprise*, 4; "Racial 'Mote' in Eye of North Gets Attention," *Baton Rouge Morning Advocate*, 12; "Look North as Well as South, Clergyman Urges," *Asheville Citizen*, 2. All found in The Vault.

36. Ockenga, "The Christian Faces Segregation." He later updated this message and preached it in 1964 as "The Christian Citizen Looks at Integration."

37. There are more than a dozen boxes of sermon manuscripts in the Ockenga archives. See Rosell, *Surprising Work*, 80–88, for helpful commentary on some of the main themes of Ockenga's ministry.

38. Harold J. Ockenga, "Harold J. Ockenga," 27.

39. Eulogizing Ockenga in a piece for *Christianity Today*, Randall Frame characterized the pastor's preaching as addressed to the mind; Frame means that Ockenga wrote his sermons out ahead of time and then memorized them, delivering them with just his Bible in front of him. Randall Frame, "Modern Evangelicalism Mourns the Loss of One of Its Founding Fathers," *Christianity Today*, March 15, 1985, 36.

40. Ibid., 29.

41. Harold J. Ockenga, "Boston at the Crossroads," sermon preached on May 21, 1950, at Park Street Church, Park Street Church Papers.

42. Interview with Timothy Keller, May 23, 2010, Trinity Evangelical Divinity School, Deerfield, Illinois.

43. Ibid.

44. Interview with Gordon Hugenberger, December 21, 2010, Park Street Church, Boston.

45. Interview with Billy Graham, correspondence through David Bruce and William Graham Tullian Tchividjian, March 11, 2011. See also his

remarks on Ockenga following his death in *Christianity Today*, March 15, 1985, 30.

46. Ibid.

47. Ibid.

48. It was not only the church that Ockenga served. In an undated *Who's Who* application some years in the future, he listed more of his activities: Past Director, Rotary Club, Boston Director, Christian Freedom Foundation, NYC; Member of Am. Acad. Polit. Sci. Clubs; Trustee, Gordon College; Trustee, Suffolk University, 1939–49; Mem. President Truman's Clergymen's Mission to Europe, 1947, VP World Evangelical Fellowship since 1951; Director of Billy Graham Association. Married to Audrey Williamson in 1935, he had three children: Audrey Starr (Oury) in 1938, Aldryth Sabra (Molyneux) in 1943, Harold John Jr. in 1947. Harold J. Ockenga, "Who's Who application," Park Street Church Papers, The Vault.

49. Mary C. MacKenzie, "Reviewing Thirty-Two Years of Ministry," *Park Street Spire*, June 1969, Park Street Church Papers, The Vault, 22. For seventeen years, MacKenzie worked as Ockenga's secretary at Park Street.

50. Interview with Ken Swetland, December 10, 2010, Gordon-Conwell Divinity School, South Hamilton, Massachusetts.

51. Audrey Ockenga, "Thirty Years in the Ministry of Park Street Church," *Park Street Spire*, June 1969, Park Street Church Papers, The Vault, 24–27.

52. Harold J. Ockenga, "Boston Bible School," Park Street Church Papers, The Vault.

53. Harold J. Ockenga, "Pastor's report for January 11, 1944," Park Street Church Papers.

54. Gleason Archer Jr., "Report of the Assistant Minister," Annual Meeting of Park Street Church, January 22, 1946, Park Street Church Papers.

55. Ibid.

56. Harold J. Ockenga to Terrelle Crum, undated letter marked "Evening School of Bible," Park Street Church Papers, The Vault.

Chapter 3: Three Mystics, Three Skeptics, and Three Evangelicals

1. Roger A. Bruns, *Preacher: Billy Sunday and Big-Time American Evangelism* (Urbana, Ill.: Univ. of Illinois Press, 1992), 17. See also George Marsden, *Fundamentalism and American Culture: The Shaping of Twentieth-Century Evangelicalism, 1870–1925* (New York: Oxford Univ. Press, 1980), 130;

William McLoughlin, *Billy Sunday Was His Real Name* (Chicago: Univ. of Chicago Press, 1955), 44, 123.

2. For more on this mindset, see Marsden, *Fundamentalism and American Culture*, 124–31.

3. See Edward J. Larson, *Summer for the Gods: The Scopes Trial and America's Continuing Debate over Science and Religion* (New York: Basic Books, 2006); Mark Edwards, "Rethinking the Failure of Fundamentalist Political Antievolutionism after 1925," *Fides et Historia* 32, no. 2: 89–106.

4. For more on Darrow, see John Aloysius Farrell, *Clarence Darrow: Attorney for the Damned* (New York: Doubleday, 2011). On Bryan, see Michael Kazin, *A Godly Hero: The Life of William Jennings Bryan* (New York: Doubleday, 2007).

5. Larson, *Summer for the Gods*, 189.

6. Marion Elizabeth Rodgers, *Mencken: The American Iconoclast; The Life and Times of the Bad Boy of Baltimore* (Oxford: Oxford Univ. Press, 2005), 293.

7. Ironically, though Mencken called Bryan "a peasant come home to the dung-pile," Bryan was in fact a wealthy man, much wealthier than Mencken.

8. Bruns, *Preacher*, 291.

9. Ibid., 294.

10. Joel Carpenter, *Revive Us Again: The Reawakening of American Fundamentalism* (New York: Oxford Univ. Press, 1997), 20.

11. Ibid., 21.

12. Virginia Lieson Brereton, *Training God's Army: The American Bible School, 1880–1940* (Bloomington, Ind.: Indiana Univ. Press, 1990), 69.

13. Ibid., 87–88.

14. John R. Rice, *I Am a Fundamentalist* (Murfreesboro, Tenn.: Sword of the Lord, 1975), 14.

15. For a fuller listing, see Brereton, *Training God's Army*, 71–76.

16. Michael S. Hamilton, "The Fundamentalist Harvard: Wheaton College and the Continuing Vitality of American Evangelicalism, 1919–1965" (PhD diss., University of Notre Dame, 1995), 168.

17. Carpenter, *Revive Us Again*, 191. The following presents the PhD attained by each scholar: Schultz, ThD in Old Testament from Harvard Divinity School (1947); Kantzer, ThD in Philosophy of Religion, HDS (1950); Tenney, PhD in Patristic and Biblical Greek, HDS (1944); Gerstner, PhD in Philosophy of Religion, HDS (1945); Goddard, ThD in Old Testament, HDS (1943); Nicole, PhD in Theology, HDS (1967; was studying for the

degree in the '40s); Crum, MA from Harvard; Carnell, PhD in Theology, HDS (1948; with a second PhD from Boston University in 1949); Archer, PhD in Classics, Harvard University (1944); Ladd, PhD in New Testament, HDS (1949); Jewett, PhD in Theology, HDS (date unknown); Henry, PhD in Philosophy of Religion, Boston University (1949). To this list we can add several more who studied at Harvard in the 1930s and '40s: Harold Lindsell, Harold Kuhn, Harold Greenlee, Glenn Barker, George Turner, Stanley Horton, John Huffman, and Lemoyne Lewis.

18. Rudolph Nelson, *The Making and Unmaking of an Evangelical Mind* (Cambridge: Cambridge Univ. Press, 1987), 56.

19. Kenneth Kantzer, "Carl Ferdinand Howard Henry: An Appreciation," in *God and Culture: Essays in Honor of Carl F. H. Henry*, ed. D. A. Carson and John D. Woodbridge (Grand Rapids: Eerdmans; London, Penn.: Paternoster, 1993), 370.

20. Ibid. In his draft of the chapter, Kantzer had written the sentence this way: "There had not been many of that kind around since Walter Maier, the Lutheran evangelist from Concordia Seminary, who had flunked out of his Old Testament program at Harvard some time back." Kantzer crossed out "flunked out of" and wrote "secured" on the draft, correcting a factual error. Kantzer Papers.

21. See Nelson, *Making and Unmaking*, 57.

22. Morton Keller and Phyllis Keller, *Making Harvard Modern: The Rise of America's University* (New York: Oxford Univ. Press, 2001), 124.

23. Ibid., 124–25.

24. Samuel Eliot Morrison, *Three Centuries of Harvard, 1636–1936* (Cambridge: Harvard Univ. Press, 1936), 395.

25. Kantzer, "Carl Ferdinand Howard Henry," 370.

26. Nelson, *Making and Unmaking*, 58–59.

27. Hamilton, "The Fundamentalist Harvard," 173–74.

28. Kantzer, "Carl Ferdinand Howard Henry," 371.

29. For more on the NAE, see Arthur Matthews, *Standing Up, Standing Together: The Emergence of the National Association of Evangelicals* (Carol Stream, Ill.: National Association of Evangelicals, 1992); James DeForest Murch, *Cooperation without Compromise: A History of the National Association of Evangelicals* (Grand Rapids: Eerdmans, 1956).

30. Kenneth Kantzer, "What ought we to expect from our church officers?" sermon on 1 Tim 3:1–12 and Titus 2:1–8, Kantzer Papers, 6.

31. Kenneth Kantzer, untitled document, Kantzer Papers.

32. Kenneth Kantzer, "For Terry Muck," Kantzer Papers, 5–6.

33. Kantzer, "Carl Ferdinand Howard Henry," 371.

34. Kenneth Kantzer, folder marked "N.T. Introduction to Cadbury II Acts to Revelation," Kantzer Papers.

35. Kenneth Kantzer, folder marked "Systematic Theology—Auer," Kantzer Papers.

36. Kenneth Kantzer, "Hackett's Questionaire—K.K.'s Statement." He crossed out "virtually fits" and wrote in "vertically fits" as seen above.

37. For more on Henry's background, see Carl F. H. Henry, *Confessions of a Theologian: An Autobiography* (Dallas: Word, 1986), 1–60. On Carnell's, see Nelson, *Making and Unmaking*, 1–48.

38. For more on Gordon Clark's life and thought, see Ronald A. Nash, ed., *The Philosophy of Gordon H. Clark: A Festschrift* (Philadelphia: P&R, 1968); Gary Crampton, *The Scriptualism of Gordon Clark* (Unicoi, Tenn.: Trinity Foundation, 1995).

39. Hamilton, "The Fundamentalist Harvard," 146. Other students mentored or tutored by Clark included Edmund Clowney, Lars Granberg, John Graybill, and fellow Cambridge evangelicals Paul Jewett and Harold Lindsell.

40. Edward John Carnell to Carl Henry, November 20, 1943, Henry Papers.

41. Ibid.

42. Ibid., March 4, 1944.

43. Edward John Carnell did not end up applying to Penn. He wanted to go to Harvard most of any school. He was so excited about Harvard that in January 1944 he actually proposed a new doctoral program in the history and philosophy of religion, a bumptious move considering he was not even accepted as a PhD student. See Nelson, *Making and Unmaking*, 52.

44. Edward John Carnell to Carl Henry, February 12, 1946.

45. Ibid.

46. Ibid., June 13, 1946.

47. Ibid., June 16, 1946.

48. Ibid., November 23, 1946.

49. Ibid., November 28, 1946.

50. Ibid., December 4, 1947.

51. Edward John Carnell to Harold J. Ockenga, September 12, 1947, Ockenga Papers.

52. Ibid.

53. Ibid., December 15, 1947.

54. Ibid., March 4, 1948.

55. Ibid., March 16, 1948.

56. Ibid.

57. Press release, December 1947, Henry Papers.

58. Edward John Carnell to Carl Henry, December 16, 1947, Henry Papers.

59. Ibid., December 23, 1947.

60. See E. J. Carnell, "The Concept of Dialectic in the Theology of Reinhold Niebuhr" (PhD diss., Harvard Divinity School, 1948).

61. See E. J. Carnell, "The Problem of Verification in Soren Kierkegaard" (PhD diss., Boston University, 1949). According to Nelson, Carnell faced an uphill climb in simultaneously carrying out "teaching responsibilities and his scholarly writing" even as he studied "for exams and [began] research on Kierkegaard for the dissertation" (75). All went well, however. Coincidentally, Henry and Carnell both mailed in their dissertation outlines on the same day, had the same second reader, and took their oral examinations back-to-back at BU on May 2, 1949. In his autobiography, Henry noted that the night before their exams, the two professors "stayed in New York overnight, and at the Sloan house YMCA to save money. But it was a terribly noisy night and neither of us got much sleep." Henry, *Confessions*, 122. Nonetheless, they passed their exams.

62. Carnell, *The Theology of Reinhold Niebuhr* (Grand Rapids, Eerdmans, 1950); Carnell, *The Burden of Søren Kierkegaard* (Grand Rapids: Eerdmans, 1956). The first was a revision of Carnell's Harvard thesis, the second a revision of his Boston University thesis.

63. John A. D'Elia, *A Place at the Table: George Eldon Ladd and the Rehabilitation of Evangelical Scholarship in America* (New York: Oxford Univ. Press, 2008), 23.

64. Ibid.

65. George Eldon Ladd to Harold J. Ockenga, October 29, 1949, Ockenga Papers.

66. Ibid.

67. Ibid.

68. Ibid.

69. Harold J. Ockenga to George Eldon Ladd, April 10, 1950, Ockenga Papers.

70. Ibid.

71. D'Elia shows that George Eldon had indeed established himself as a

leading American scholar of the New Testament, regardless of worldview. Tragically, Ladd could not—or would not—recognize this. See D'Elia, *A Place at the Table*, 91–119.

Chapter 4: Grand Strategy by the Beach

1. Projects that have taken note of this convergence to one degree or another include Rudolph Nelson, *The Making and Unmaking of an Evangelical Mind* (Cambridge: Cambridge Univ. Press, 1987), 54–72; Joel Carpenter, *Revive Us Again: The Reawakening of American Fundamentalism* (New York: Oxford Univ. Press, 1997), 190–94; Mark Noll, *Between Faith and Criticism: Evangelicals, Scholarship, and the Bible* (San Francisco: Harper and Row, 1987), 94–99; John A. D'Elia, *A Place at the Table: George Eldon Ladd and the Rehabilitation of Evangelical Scholarship in America* (Oxford: Oxford Univ. Press, 2008), 22–23; D. G. Hart, *Deconstructing Evangelicalism: Protestant Christianity in the Age of Billy Graham* (Grand Rapids: Baker, 2004), 134–35; Glenn T. Miller, *Piety and Profession: American Protestant Theological Education, 1870–1970* (Grand Rapids, Eerdmans, 2007), 634; David Lee Russell, "Coming to Grips with the Age of Reason: An Analysis of the New Evangelical Intellectual Agenda, 1942–1970" (PhD diss., Michigan State University, 1993), 67–68. As noted previously, all of this scholarship is dependent on Nelson's original research.

2. Harold J. Ockenga, *These Religious Affections* (Grand Rapids: Zondervan, 1937); *Our Protestant Heritage* (Grand Rapids: Zondervan, 1938); *Have You Met These Women?* (Grand Rapids: Zondervan, 1940); *Every One That Believeth* (New York: Revell, 1942); *The Comfort of God* (New York: Revell, 1944); *The Spirit of the Living God* (New York: Revell, 1947); *Faithful in Christ Jesus* (New York: Revell, 1948).

3. Garth M. Rosell, *The Surprising Work of God: Harold John Ockenga, Billy Graham, and the Rebirth of Evangelicalism* (Grand Rapids: Baker, 2008), 86.

4. It was reputed that Park Street supported as many missionaries as any other church in America. See Harold Lindsell, *Park Street Prophet: A Life of Harold John Ockenga* (Wheaton, Ill.: Van Kampen, 1951), 171.

5. The extant scholarly coverage is limited to Rosell, *Surprising Work*, 197–201; Donald MacLeod, *C. Stacey Woods and the Evangelical Rediscovery of the University* (Downers Grove, Ill.: InterVarsity, 2007), 17–19.

6. Harold J. Ockenga, foreword to *The Battle for the Bible*, by Harold Lindsell (Grand Rapids: Zondervan, 1976), 11. Interestingly, Ockenga omits the 1947 conference, though it is not clear why.

7. Harold J. Ockenga, "First Meeting of Evangelical Scholars," Ockenga Papers.

8. Ibid.

9. Harold J. Ockenga, "New Defence of Christian Faith Charted," Ockenga Papers.

10. Harold J. Ockenga to Carl Henry, June 8, 1945, Ockenga Papers.

11. Report of the Second Annual Conference for the Advancement of Evangelical Scholarship," Ockenga Papers.

12. Ibid.

13. Ibid.

14. Ibid.

15. Ibid.

16. Ibid.

17. Ibid.

18. Ibid.

19. Harold J. Ockenga to Terrelle B. Crum, April 2, 1947, Ockenga Papers.

20. Ibid.

21. Harold J. Ockenga to Carl Henry, January 8, 1947, Ockenga Papers.

22. Carl Henry to Harold J. Ockenga, January 27, 1947, Ockenga Papers. Henry makes brief mention of the 1947 gathering in *Confessions of a Theologian: An Autobiography* (Dallas: Word, 1986), 113.

23. John Bolten was a businessman from Germany who came to Boston following early Nazi persecution. He lost his fortune but eventually built it back and became a major supporter of Billy Graham, Ockenga, and other Christian leaders. Bolten generously financed all three conferences, totaling a major expenditure and highlighting the highly strategic role such a financier can play in Christian work. See Rosell, *Suprising Work*, 197n38; Billy Graham, *Just As I Am: The Autobiography of Billy Graham* (San Francisco: HarperSanFrancisco; Grand Rapids: Zondervan, 1997), 168–71.

24. Joseph Free to Harold J. Ockenga, May 17, 1947, Ockenga Papers.

25. Edward John Carnell to Harold J. Ockenga, March 31, 1947, Ockenga Papers.

26. Ibid.

27. See Edward John Carnell to Harold J. Ockenga, March 31, 1947, Ockenga Papers; John Woodbridge and Wendy Murray Zoba, "Standing on the Promises: Interview with Carl Henry and Kenneth Kantzer," *Christianity Today*, September 16, 1996, 33.

28. Abraham Kuyper, "Sphere Sovereignty," in *Abraham Kuyper: A Centennial*

Reader, ed. James D. Bratt (Grand Rapids: Eerdmans, 1998), 488. See also James D. Bratt, *Abraham Kuyper: Modern Calvinist, Christian Democrat* (Grand Rapids: Eerdmans, 2013).

29. See Molly Worthen, *Apostles of Reason: The Crisis of Authority in American Evangelicalism* (New York: Oxford Univ. Press, 2013), 58.

30. Harold J. Ockenga to Terrelle B. Crum, April 2, 1947, Ockenga Papers.

31. "Conference for Advancement of Evangelical Scholarship," June 23–27, 1947, Ockenga Papers.

32. Harold J. Ockenga to Terrelle B. Crum, April 2, 1947, Ockenga Papers.

33. Rosell, *Surprising Work*, 201.

34. Harold J. Ockenga to Carl Henry, June 8, 1945, Ockenga Papers.

35. Henry, *Confessions of a Theologian*, 105.

36. Ibid., xxi.

37. Edward John Carnell to Carl Henry, December 4, 1947, Henry Papers.

38. Harold Lindsell, "Harold John Ockenga: The Park Street Prophet," *Christianity Today*, March 15, 1985, 36.

39. Lindsell, *Park Street Prophet*, 89.

40. Kenneth Kantzer, *Christianity Today*, November 6, 1981, 1.

41. Carl F. H. Henry, *Gods of This Age . . . or God of the Ages?* ed. R. Albert Mohler Jr. (Nashville: Broadman and Holman, 1994), 112. The original lecture, titled "The Shrouded Peaks of Learning," was given at a 1988 conference in Oxford on the state of the Christian mind. See Carl Henry to Craig Tavani, April 8, 1988, Henry Papers. The text cited above is a collection of many of Henry's lectures and addresses.

42. Carl Henry to Fuller Theological Seminary faculty, January 23, 1955, Henry Papers.

43. John A. Huffman, interview by Robert Shuster, 1988, Tapes 1–5, Huffman Papers, Wheaton College, Wheaton, Illinois.

44. Ibid.

45. Ibid.

Chapter 5: Acts of Intellectual Daring

1. Find this and other resources from the program at *http://new.ofrh.com/radio/salvation-invitation*.

2. Interview with Daniel Fuller by correspondence, March 11, 2011.

3. For more on Charles Fuller's background, see Daniel P. Fuller, *Give the Winds a Mighty Voice: The Story of Charles E. Fuller* (Waco: Word,

1972), 11–116; Joel A. Carpenter, *Revive Us Again: The Reawakening of American Fundamentalism* (Oxford: Oxford Univ. Press, 1997), 135–40; George Marsden, *Reforming Fundamentalism: Fuller Seminary and the New Evangelicalism* (Grand Rapids: Eerdmans, 1987), 13–23.

4. Fuller, *Give the Winds*, 211.

5. Harold J. Ockenga, "Challenge to the Christian Civilization of the West," Ockenga Papers; Carl F. H. Henry, *The Uneasy Conscience of Modern Fundamentalism*, ed. Richard Mouw (1947; repr., Grand Rapids: Eerdmans, 2003).

6. Harold J. Ockenga to Charles E. Fuller, October 31, 1946, Ockenga Papers.

7. Interview with Daniel Fuller by correspondence, March 11, 2011.

8. Fuller, *Give the Winds* , 200.

9. Harold J. Ockenga to Charles E. Fuller, March 12, 1947, Ockenga Papers.

10. Ibid., May 2, 1947.

11. Ibid., May 8, 1947.

12. Ibid., May 24, 1947.

13. Ibid., November 19, 1947.

14. For more on the school's first faculty, see Marsden, *Reforming Fundamentalism*, 25–27.

15. Harold J. Ockenga to Charles E. Fuller, October 25, 1947, Ockenga Papers.

16. George Marsden has chronicled the early days of the school. See chapter 3, "Rebuilding Western Civilization," in Marsden, *Reforming Fundamentalism*, 53–68.

17. Harold J. Ockenga, "Theological Education," Ockenga Papers.

18. Harold J. Ockenga, "Challenge to the Christian Civilization of the West," Ockenga Papers.

19. Bill Bright did not last long at Fuller, but before he left, his ministry was named by Fuller professor Wilbur Smith. See John G. Turner, *Bill Bright and Campus Crusade for Christ: The Renewal of Evangelicalism in Postwar America* (Chapel Hill: Univ. of North Carolina Press, 2008), 37–38.

20. Marsden, *Reforming Fundamentalism*, 61.

21. This message is found in Russell Spittler, ed., *Fuller Voices: Then and Now* (Pasadena, Calif.: Fuller Seminary Press, 2004).

22. Carl Henry, "Summary of Address by Carl F. H. Henry," foreword to "Challenge to the Christian Civilization," by Ockenga.

23. Ockenga, "Challenge to the Christian Civilization," 2.

24. Ibid.

25. Ibid., 3.

26. Ibid., 4.

27. Ibid., 5.

28. Ibid., 7.

29. Ibid., 9.

30. Ibid.

31. Ibid.

32. Ibid., 10.

33. Henry, *Uneasy Conscience.*

34. Ockenga was not hostile toward fundamentalists, however. In a later essay, he stated that while there was something "wrong with the fundamentalist strategy" such that "the fundamentalists were not Christian in their attitude of defending the faith," it was also true that "[f]undamentalists were noble men, committed to orthodox Christianity, who suffered at the hands of ecclesiastical modernism. They were discriminated against, ostracized, persecuted, and ridiculed. One can sympathize, understand, and exonerate these faithful men for their willingness to contend against the liberals." These words, penned thirty years after the Fuller commencement, suggest something of a softening in Ockenga's conception of the fundamentalists. Harold J. Ockenga, "From Fundamentalism, Through New Evangelicalism, to Evangelicalism," in *Evangelical Roots: A Tribute to Wilbur Smith*, ed. Kenneth Kantzer (Nashville: Thomas Nelson, 1978), 42. Kantzer offered additional commentary on Ockenga's early interactions with fundamentalism in an unpublished documentary fragment: "Ockenga claims to have coined the term Neo-Evangelical in order to show that he was not a Fundamentalist in the 'bad' sense. He believed the original Fundamentals, so he argued, but he did not stand for many things characteristic of Fundamentalists in general. Chiefly, he wished to put himself in another class from the anti-denominational Fundamentalists and separatist Fundamentalists. Starting Fuller, he wanted to feed students into the denominations and tarred with the brush of Fundamentalism, most large denominations were afraid of Fuller men. If they could be known not as Fundamentalists *(generally separatistic), his students would much more likely find acceptance within liberal denominations."* This understanding of Ockenga as attempting to distance himself from a "bad" form of fundamentalism fits with how Henry and Kantzer saw themselves in relation to the fundamentalist movement. Kenneth Kantzer, "The New Evangelicalism—Extension Service," Kantzer Papers.

35. Kenneth Kantzer, undated sermon titled "Premillennialism," Kantzer Papers.

36. See David O. Beale, *In Pursuit of Purity: American Fundamentalism Since 1850* (Greenville, S.C.: Unusual, 1986), 246ff.; George W. Dollar, *A History of Fundamentalism in America* (Greenville, S.C.: Bob Jones, 1973), 250–80; George Marsden, *Understanding Fundamentalism and Evangelicalism* (Grand Rapids: Eerdmans, 1991), 98–120; F. Lionel Young III, "To the Right of Billy Graham: John R. Rice's 1957 Crusade against New Evangelicalism and the End of the Fundamentalist-Evangelical Coalition" (ThM thesis, Trinity Evangelical Divinity School, 2005).

37. Henry, *Uneasy Conscience*, 65.

38. Ibid., 68.

39. Ibid.

40. Ibid., 69.

41. D. G. Hart, *That Old-Time Religion in Modern America: Evangelical Protestantism in the Twentieth Century* (Chicago: Ivan Dee, 2002), 125.

42. "The Evangelical Theological Society," Henry Papers.

43. Ibid.

44. Carl Henry, "Fifty Years of American Theology and the Contemporary Need," *Calvin Forum*, February 1950, Henry Papers.

45. Hart, *That Old-Time Religion*, 126.

46. "Evangelical Theologians Set Up Scholarly Body," *United Evangelical Action*, January 1950.

47. Membership Records of the Evangelical Theological Society, 1952, Henry Papers.

48. Roger Nicole, interview by John Muether, Spring 2008, Reformed Theological Seminary, Orlando; *http://www.rts.edu/Site/Resources/M-L/docs/Nicole_Interview_MLSpring08.pdf* (accessed on April 25, 2011).

49. Ibid., 129.

50. Billy Graham, *Just as I Am: The Autobiography of Billy Graham* (San Francisco: HarperSanFrancisco; Grand Rapids: Zondervan, 1997), 286.

51. The initial investment was twenty-five thousand dollars from Pew; many hundreds of thousands would follow over the years. See Graham, *Just as I Am*, 288.

52. Wilbur Smith, one of Henry's founding faculty colleagues at Fuller, was Graham's first choice for the editorship. Smith wept when Graham offered him the job but soon declined. Ibid., 287.

53. *Christianity Today*, March 31, 1958, 2.

54. Carl Henry to Paul S. Rees, November 14, 1956, Henry Papers.

55. Ibid.

56. "Reader Approval! *Christianity Today Tops Opinion Research Poll of Eleven Leading Religious Magazines*," Henry Papers.

Chapter 6: Carl Henry's University Crusade

1. For more on the impact of this statement, see Billy Graham, *Just as I Am: The Autobiography of Billy Graham* (San Francisco: HarperSanFrancisco; Grand Rapids: Zondervan, 1997), 149–50.

2. Billy Graham was named by United Airlines the most traveled civilian passenger in America in 1945–46. In 1945 alone he traveled to forty-seven states. Joel Carpenter, *Revive Us Again: The Reawakening of American Fundamentalism* (New York: Oxford Univ. Press, 1997), 217.

3. Carl Henry to Billy Graham, October 8, 1955, Henry Papers.

4. Ibid.

5. Ibid.

6. Ibid.

7. Billy Graham to Carl Henry, October 15, 1955, Henry Papers.

8. Ibid.

9. Carl Henry to Billy Graham, October 16, 1955, Henry Papers.

10. Billy Graham was nothing if not a skilled visionary and entrepreneur. See Grant Wacker, *America's Pastor: Billy Graham and the Shaping of a Nation* (Cambridge: Belknap, 2014), chap. 4.

11. Carl Henry to Billy Graham, October 16, 1955, Henry Papers.

12. Ibid.

13. Ibid.

14. Carl Henry to John H. Strong, December 16, 1955, Henry Papers.

15. Carl Henry to Billy Graham, December 22, 1955, Henry Papers.

16. "Personnel November 5, 1959 meeting concerning crusade University," Henry Papers. Attendees are listed as they are recognized in the document.

17. "A Time for Decision in Higher Education," Henry Papers.

18. "Crisis," Crusade University booklet, Henry Papers.

19. "Objectives," Crusade University booklet, Henry Papers.

20. "Control," Crusade University booklet, Henry Papers.

21. "Location," Crusade University booklet, Henry Papers.

22. See Curtis Mitchell, *God in the Garden: The Story of the Billy Graham New York Crusade* (New York: Doubleday, 1957).

23. "Goodbye Billy," *New York Journal-American*, September 4, 1957.

24. Graham, *Just As I Am*, 323.

25. "Faculty," Crusade University booklet, Henry Papers.

26. "Costs," Crusade University booklet, Henry Papers. The booklet listed the tuition costs of twenty universities in 1959–60, including Harvard $1,250, Amherst $1,050, Princeton $1,450, and Swarthmore $1,250. The average tuition for the group of schools was $1,229.

27. "Proposed Budget," Crusade University booklet, Henry Papers.

28. Henry's "Paragraph B" reference suggested that "Graduate and specialized training could be added to existing programs of accredited Christian colleges if adequate financing were provided." Carl Henry, "Report to the Steering Committee," Henry Papers.

29. Henry, "Report to the Steering Committee."

30. For more on the initial meeting, see Garth M. Rosell, *The Surprising Work of God: Harold John Ockenga, Billy Graham, and the Rebirth of Evangelicalism* (Grand Rapids: Baker, 2008), 208–9.

31. John McCandless Phillips, "Protestants Map University Here," *New York Times*, May 5, 1960, A5.

32. Ibid.

33. Carl F. H. Henry, "Why a Christian University?" *Christianity Today*, October 10, 1960, 24.

34. Ibid.

35. "Consultation on a Christian University," Sheraton Park Hotel, Washington, DC, November 4–5, 1960, Henry Papers. Attendees are listed as they were identified in this document.

36. Carl F. H. Henry, *Christian Personal Ethics* (Grand Rapids: Eerdmans, 1957).

37. Untitled document, Henry Papers.

38. Carl Henry, "Toward a Christian University," Henry Papers.

39. Carl Henry to S. H. Mullen, September 25, 1962, Henry Papers.

40. Rosell, *Surprising Work*, 210–11.

41. Daniel Poling, *Why Billy Graham?* (Santa Fe, N.M.: Sunstone Press, 2008), 70–72.

42. Carl Henry to William Schmidt Jr., November 12, 1962, Henry Papers.

43. Carl Henry to Billy Graham, February 23, 1965, Henry Papers.

44. Carl Henry to Alan R. Bell, August 20, 1965, Henry Papers.

45. Ibid.

46. Ibid.

47. Carl F. H. Henry, *Confessions of a Theologian: An Autobiography* (Dallas: Word, 1986), 341.

48. "Educators Endorse Institute Plan: Action Committee Named to Project Institute for Advanced Christian Studies," *Christianity Today*, February 17, 1967, 508.

49. See "IFACS Dissolves," *Conference on Faith and History* 8 (2003): 8.

50. Carl Henry, *Confessions*, 340–41. See Samuel Hugh Moffett, *A History of Christianity in Asia: Beginnings to 1500* (Maryknoll, N.Y.: Orbis, 1998); Moffett, *A History of Christianity in Asia: Volume II 1500–1900*, American Society of Missiology Series 36 (Maryknoll, N.Y.: Orbis, 2005); Nicholas Wolterstorff, *Art in Action: Toward a Christian Aesthetic* (Grand Rapids: Eerdmans, 1980).

51. Ibid., 342.

52. Ibid.

53. Carl Henry to Harold J. Ockenga, February 16, 1966, Henry Papers.

54. "Wheaton President Proposes Cooperative National University," April 1966, Wheaton College News Service, Henry Papers.

55. Carl Henry to Hudson Armerding, October 6, 1966, Henry Papers.

56. "A Proposal for a Cluster College Campus," Henry Papers.

57. Carl Henry, Presentation given on June 23, 1983, at the Mayflower Hotel in Washington, DC, Henry Papers.

58. Carl Henry to Craig Tavani, April 8, 1988, Henry Papers.

59. Carl Henry to T. Grady Spires, August 22, 1989, Henry Papers.

60. Kenneth Kantzer, "The Carl Henry That Might Have Been," *Christianity Today*, April 5, 1993.

61. Ibid.

Conclusion

1. Harold J. Ockenga, foreword to *The Battle for the Bible*, by Harold Lindsell (Grand Rapids: Zondervan, 1976), 9–10.

2. Harold J. Ockenga to Edward John Carnell, August 17, 1961, Ockenga Papers.

3. Ibid., July 31, 1961.

4. Edward John Carnell to Harold J. Ockenga, January 7, 1964, Ockenga Papers.

5. My interpretation of Carnell's death is based in my own study, which includes secondhand reports of Carnell's health during his final years from John Woodbridge of Trinity Evangelical Divinity School. My understanding of Carnell, based in considerable measure on the extensive Ockenga-Carnell correspondence, differs from the presentation of him in Rudolph Nelson, *The Making and Unmaking of an Evangelical Mind* (Cambridge: Cambridge Univ. Press, 1987), though I appreciate numerous facets of Nelson's work.

6. Henry did believe, however, that he and Carnell offered such significant contribution to the guild that they made the "reemergence of evangelical systematic theology" the most significant development in postwar American theology. See Carl F. H. Henry, *Gods of This Age . . . or God of the Ages?* ed. R. Albert Mohler Jr. (Nashville: Broadman and Holman, 1994), 112.

7. Ibid.

8. "Biography," 496.

9. Ibid., 497.

10. Interview with D. A. Carson, April 15, 2008, Trinity Evangelical Divinity School, Deerfield, Illinois.

11. Mark Dever, correspondence with the author, December 17, 2014.

12. John A. D'Elia, *A Place at the Table: George Eldon Ladd and the Rehabilitation of Evangelical Scholarship in America* (New York: Oxford Univ. Press, 2008), 149ff.

13. Ibid., 182.

14. John Adams, "The Making of a Neo-Evangelical Statesman: The Case of Harold John Ockenga" (PhD diss., Baylor University, 1994), 150ff. See also The Harold John Ockenga Institute at Gordon-Conwell Theological Seminary, found online at *http://www.gordonconwell.edu/resources/ockenga.cfm*. The site is so extensive as to helpfully include proper pronunciation of Ockenga's name.

15. John Piper, "The Pastor as Scholar," in *The Pastor as Scholar and the Scholar as Pastor: Reflections on Life and Ministry,* John Piper and D. A. Carson, ed. Owen Strachan and David Mathis (Carol Stream, Ill.: Crossway, 2011), 36.

16. Ibid., 36–47.

17. See Collin Hansen, *Young, Restless, Reformed: A Journalist's Travels with the New Calvinists* (Carol Stream, Ill.: Crossway, 2009).

18. Interview with Wayne Grudem, electronic correspondence, March 31, 2011.

19. Wayne Grudem, *Systematic Theology: An Introduction to Biblical Doctrine* (1994; repr., Grand Rapids: Zondervan, 2010).

20. Roger Nicole, "What Evangelicalism Has Accomplished," *Christianity Today*, September 16, 1996, 32.

21. Ibid, 33.

22. Ibid., 32.

23. Alan Wolfe, "Opening of the Evangelical Mind," *Atlantic Monthly*, October 2000.

24. Richard Mouw, "Ultimately Everything Holds Together," *Atlantic Monthly* online, October 2000.

25. Neil Gross and Solon Simmons, "The Religiosity of American College and University Professors," *Sociology of Religion*, January 1, 2009. Referenced online on December 13, 2013 at *doi:10.1093/socrel/srp026*.

26. See the data on the CCCU at *http://en.wikipedia.org/wiki/Council_for_Christian_Colleges_and_Universities*.

27. Molly Worthen, *Apostles of Reason: The Crisis of Authority in American Evangelicalism* (New York: Oxford Univ. Press, 2013), 261.

28. I appreciate Matthew Avery Sutton's recent work, but I believe that the matter of institutions allow for much greater distinction between fundamentalists and evangelicals than Sutton suggests. It is quite right that these groups had widespread theological agreement. But we cannot leave the matter there; we must, as this book has attempted to do, include in our intellectual history of neo-evangelicalism a properly social or, we could say, institutional history. It is at this point, I posit, that we see the great divergence between the fundamentalists and the evangelicals, for the two groups held wildly different institutional and cooperational visions. We thus must be careful not to overemphasize the continuities between these sectors of American Christianity. See Matthew Avery Sutton, *American Apocalypse: A History of Modern Evangelicalism* (Cambridge, Mass.: Harvard University Press, 2014), 373.

29. Mark Noll, *The Scandal of the Evangelical Mind* (Grand Rapids: Eerdmans, 1995), 3.

30. Mark Noll, *Jesus Christ and the Life of the Mind* (Grand Rapids: Eerdmans, 2011), 165.

31. For a compelling summary of the fault lines in American culture and society, see George Marsden, *The Twilight of the American Enlightenment: The 1950s and the Crisis of Liberal Belief* (New York: Basic Books, 2013).

BIBLIOGRAPHY

Abell, Aaron. *The Urban Impact on American Protestantism, 1865–1900.* Cambridge, Mass.: Harvard Univ. Press, 1943.

Adams, John. "The Making of a Neo-Evangelical Statesman: The Case of Harold John Ockenga." PhD diss., Baylor University, 1994.

Anonymous. "Legislators Weigh Fate of Pitt Gift." *The Pittsburgh Press,* May 12, 1935, 1.

Anonymous. "Return of the Prophet." *Time,* March 13, 1946, 25.

Balmer, Randall. *Encyclopedia of Evangelicalism.* Waco, Tex.: Baylor Univ. Press, 2004.

Bendroth, Margaret Lamberts. *Fundamentalists in the City: Conflict and Division in Boston's Churches, 1885–1950.* Oxford: Oxford Univ. Press, 2005.

Brereton, Virginia Lieson. *Training God's Army: The American Bible School, 1880–1940.* Bloomington, Ind.: Indiana Univ. Press, 1990.

Bruns, Roger A. *Preacher: Billy Sunday and Big-Time American Evangelism.* Urbana, Ill.: Univ. of Illinois, 1992.

Burch, Maxie. *The Evangelical Historians: The Historiography of George Marsden, Nathan Hatch, and Mark Noll.* Lanham, Md.: University Press of America, 2002.

Bush, L. Russ, and Thomas Nettles. *Baptists and the Bible.* 1980; Nashville: Broadman and Holman Academic, 1999.

Carpenter, Joel A., ed. *A New Evangelical Coalition.* New York: Garland, 1988.

———. *Revive Us Again: The Reawakening of American Fundamentalism.* New York: Oxford Univ. Press, 1997.

———. *Two Reformers of Fundamentalism: Harold John Ockenga and Carl F. H. Henry.* New York: Garland, 1988.

Carson, D. A., and John D. Woodbridge, eds. *God and Culture: Essays in*

Honor of Carl F. H. Henry. Grand Rapids: Eerdmans; London: Paternoster, 1993.

———. Interview with author. Deerfield, Illinois, April 15, 2011.

Crisler, A. R. "Circus of Superlatives." *New York Times*, January 7, 1940.

Dayton, Donald W. *Discovering an Evangelical Heritage.* New York: Harper and Row, 1976.

D'Elia, John A. *A Place at the Table: George Eldon Ladd and the Rehabilitation of Evangelical Scholarship in America.* New York: Oxford Univ. Press, 2008.

Dochuk, Darren. *From Bible Belt to Sunbelt: Plain-Folk Religion, Grassroots Politics, and the Rise of Evangelical Conservatism.* New York: Norton, 2011.

Dorrien, Gary. *The Making of American Liberal Theology: Imagining Progressive Religion, 1805–1900.* Louisville: Westminster John Knox, 2001.

Dorsett, Lyle. *Billy Sunday and the Redemption of Urban America.* Grand Rapids: Eerdmans, 1991.

Doyle, G. Wright. *Carl Henry: Theologian for All Seasons.* Eugene, Ore.: Pickwick, 2010.

Edwards, Mark. "Rethinking the Failure of Fundamentalist Political Antievolutionism after 1925." *Fides et Historia* 32, no. 2: 89–106.

Englizian, H. Crosby. *Brimstone Corner: Park Street Church, Boston.* Chicago: Moody, 1968.

Eskridge, Larry, and Mark A. Noll. *More Money, More Ministry: Money and Evangelicals in Recent North American History.* Grand Rapids: Eerdmans, 2000.

Finstuen, Andrew. *Original Sin and Everyday Protestants: The Theology of Reinhold Niebuhr, Billy Graham, and Paul Tillich in an Age of Anxiety.* Chapel Hill: Univ. of North Carolina, 2009.

Frame, Randall. "Modern Evangelicalism Mourns the Loss of One of Its Founding Fathers." *Christianity Today*, March 15, 1985, 29–30.

Fuller, Daniel P. *Give the Winds a Mighty Voice: The Story of Charles E. Fuller.* Dallas: Word, 1972.

Gabbert, M. R. "Moral Freedom." *The Journal of Philosophy* 24, no. 17 (1927): 464–72.

———. *A Series of Six Radio Talks on Conversations with a Philosopher.* Pittsburgh: Univ. of Pittsburgh, 1925.

Gasaway, Brantley W. *Progressive Evangelicals and the Pursuit of Social Justice.* Chapel Hill, NC: University of North Carolina Press, 2014.

Gloege, Timothy. "Consumed: Reuben A. Torrey and the Creation of Corporate Fundamentalism, 1880–1930." PhD diss., University of Notre Dame, 2006.

Graham, Billy. "Harold John Ockenga: A Man Who Walked with God." *Christianity Today*, March 15, 1985, 30.

———. *Just As I Am: The Autobiography of Billy Graham.* San Francisco: HarperSanFrancisco; Grand Rapids: Zondervan, 1997.

Grudem, Wayne. Interview with author. Electronic correspondence. March 15, 2011.

Hamilton, Michael S. "The Fundamentalist Harvard: Wheaton College and the Continuing Vitality of American Evangelicalism, 1919–1965." PhD diss., University of Notre Dame, 1995.

Hankins, Barry. *Francis Shaeffer and the Shaping of Evangelical America.* Library of Religious Biography Series. Grand Rapids: Eerdmans, 2008.

Hannah, John D. *An Uncommon Union: Dallas Theological Seminary and American Evangelicalism.* Grand Rapids: Zondervan, 2009.

Hansen, Collin. *Young, Restless, Reformed: A Journalist's Travels with the New Calvinists.* Carol Stream, Ill.: Crossway, 2009.

Hart, D. G. *Deconstructing Evangelicalism: Protestant Christianity in the Age of Billy Graham.* Grand Rapids: Baker, 2004.

———. *Defending the Faith: J. Gresham Machen and the Crisis of Conservative Protestantism in Modern America.* Baltimore: Johns Hopkins Univ. Press, 1994.

———. *Reckoning with the Past: Historical Essays on American Evangelicalism from the Institute for the Study of American Evangelicals.* Grand Rapids: Baker, 1996.

———. *That Old-Time Religion in Modern America: Evangelical Protestantism in the Twentieth Century.* Chicago: Ivan R. Dee, 2002.

Hartley, Benjamin L. *Evangelicals at Crossroads: Revivalism and Social Reform in Boston, 1860–1910.* Durham, N.H.: Univ. of New Hampshire Press, 2011.

Henry, Carl F. H. *Confessions of a Theologian: An Autobiography.* Dallas: Word, 1986.

———. *Gods of This Age . . . or God of the Ages?* Ed. R. Albert Mohler Jr. Nashville: Broadman and Holman, 1994.

———. *Remaking the Modern Mind.* Grand Rapids: Eerdmans, 1946.

———. *The Uneasy Conscience of Modern Fundamentalism.* 1947; Grand Rapids: Eerdmans, 2003.

———. "Why a Christian University?" *Christianity Today*, October 10, 1960, 24–25.

Holifield, E. Brooks. *God's Ambassadors: A History of the Christian Clergy in America*. Grand Rapids: Eerdmans, 2007.

Hope, Richard. "Mont Robertson Gabbert." *Proceedings and Addresses of the American Philosophical Association* 28 (1954–55): 62.

Hugenberger, Gordon. Interview by author. Boston, Massachusetts, December 21, 2010.

Kantzer, Kenneth. "The Carl Henry That Might Have Been." *Christianity Today*, April 5, 1993.

Kazin, Michael. *A Godly Hero: The Life of William Jennings Bryan*. New York: Doubleday, 2007.

Keller, Morton, and Phyllis Keller. *Making Harvard Modern: The Rise of America's University*. New York: Oxford Univ. Press, 2001.

Keller, Timothy. Interview by author. Deerfield, Illinois, April 23, 2010.

Kidd, Thomas. *The Great Awakening: The Roots of Evangelical Christianity in Colonial America*. New Haven, Conn.: Yale Univ. Press, 2007.

Kling, David W. *A Field of Divine Wonders: The New Divinity and Village Revivals in Northwestern Connecticut, 1792–1822*. State College, Penn.: Penn State Univ. Press, 1993.

Krapohl, Robert H., and Charles H. Lippy. *The Evangelicals: A Historical, Thematic, and Biographical Guide*. Westport, Conn.: Greenwood, 1999.

Larson, Edward J. *Summer for the Gods: The Scopes Trial and America's Continuing Debate over Science and Religion*. New York: Basic Books, 2006.

Larson, Mel. *Young Man on Fire: The Story of Torrey Johnson and Youth for Christ*. Chicago: Youth Publications, 1943.

Lean, Garth. *Frank Buchman: A Life*. London: Constable and Co., 1985.

Lindsay, D. Michael. *Faith in the Halls of Power: How Evangelicals Joined the American Elite*. New York: Oxford Univ. Press, 2007.

Lindsell, Harold. *The Battle for the Bible*. Grand Rapids: Zondervan, 1976.

———. "Harold John Ockenga: The Park Street Prophet." *Christianity Today*, March 15, 1985, 36.

———. *Park Street Prophet: A Life of Harold John Ockenga*. Wheaton, Ill.: Van Kampen, 1951.

Logan, Ernest Edwin. *The Church That Was Twice Born: A History of the First Presbyterian Church of Pittsburgh, Pennsylvania, 1773–1973*. Pittsburgh: Pickwick-Morcraft, 1973.

Longfield, Bradley J. *The Presbyterian Controversy: Fundamentalists, Modernists, and Moderates.* Religion in America. New York: Oxford Univ. Press, 1993.

Macleod, A. Donald. "A. Z. Conrad: Park Street Pioneer." *New England Reformed Journal* 16 (2000): 1–14.

———. *C. Stacey Woods and the Evangelical Rediscovery of the University.* Downers Grove, Ill.: InterVarsity, 2007.

Macrae, A. A. "Why the League." *The Evangelical Student* 1 (1926): 3–4.

Mangum, R. Todd. *The Dispensational-Covenantal Rift: The Fissuring of American Evangelical Theology from 1936–1944.* Studies in Evangelical History and Thought. Carlisle, Penn.: Paternoster, 2007.

Marsden, George M. *Fundamentalism and American Culture: The Shaping of Twentieth-Century Evangelicalism, 1870–1925.* New York: Oxford Univ. Press, 1980.

———. *Reforming Fundamentalism: Fuller Seminary and the New Evangelicalism.* Grand Rapids: Eerdmans, 1987.

———. *The Soul of the American University: From Protestant Establishment to Established Nonbelief.* New York: Oxford Univ. Press, 1996.

———. *The Twilight of the American Enlightenment: The 1950s and the Crisis of Liberal Belief.* New York: Basic Books, 2013.

———. *Understanding Fundamentalism and Evangelicalism.* Grand Rapids: Eerdmans, 1991.

Martin, David V. *Trinity International University, 1897–1997: A Century of Training Christian Leaders.* Deerfield, Ill.: Trinity International University, 1998.

Marty, Martin, ed. *Modern American Protestantism and Its World.* Vol. 10, *Fundamentalism and Evangelicalism.* Munich: Saur, 1993.

Massa, Mark S. "Mediating Modernism: Charles Briggs, Catholic Modernism, and an Ecumenical 'Plot.'" *Harvard Theological Review* 81, no. 4 (October 1988): 413–30.

Matthews, Arthur. *Standing Up, Standing Together: The Emergence of the National Association of Evangelicals.* Carol Stream, Ill.: National Association of Evangelicals, 1992.

Miller, Eric J. "Carl F. H. Henry and Christianity Today: Responding to the 'Crisis of the West,' 1956–1968." MA thesis, Trinity Evangelical Divinity School, 1994.

Miller, Glenn T. *Piety and Profession: American Protestant Theological Education, 1870–1970.* Grand Rapids: Eerdmans, 2007.

Miller, Steven P. *Billy Graham and the Rise of the Republican South.* Politics and Culture in the American South. Philadelphia: Univ. of Pennsylvania, 2009.

———. *The Age of Evangelicalism: America's Born-Again Years.* New York: Oxford University Press, 2014.

Moat, Robert Miller. *Harry Emerson Fosdick: Preacher, Pastor, Prophet.* New York: Oxford Univ. Press, 2005.

Mohler, R. Albert Jr. "Carl F. H. Henry." In *Theologians of the Baptist Tradition.* Edited by Timothy George and David S. Dockery. Nashville: Broadman and Holman, 2001.

Moore, Martin. *Boston Revival, 1842: A Brief History of the Evangelical Churches of Boston, Together with a More Particular Account of the Revival of 1842.* 1842. Reprint, Wheaton, Ill.: Richard Owen Roberts, 1980.

Morison, Samuel Eliot. *Three Centuries of Harvard, 1636–1936.* Cambridge: Harvard Univ. Press, 1936.

Mouw, Richard. *Called to the Life of the Mind: Some Advice for Evangelical Scholars.* Grand Rapids: Eerdmans, 2014.

———. *Consulting the Faithful: What Christian Intellectuals Can Learn from Popular Religion.* Grand Rapids: Eerdmans, 1994.

———. *He Shines in All That's Fair: Culture and Common Grace.* Grand Rapids: Eerdmans, 2001.

———. *The Smell of Sawdust: What Evangelicals Can Learn from Their Fundamentalist Heritage.* Grand Rapids: Zondervan, 2000.

Murch, James DeForest. *Cooperation without Compromise: A History of the National Association of Evangelicals.* Grand Rapids: Eerdmans, 1956.

Murray, Iain. *Evangelicalism Divided: A Record of Crucial Change in the Years 1950–2000.* Carlisle, Penn.: Banner of Truth, 2000.

Murray, William Henry Harrison. *The Busted Ex-Texan and Other Stories.* Boston: DeWolfe, Fiske, and Co., 1890.

———. *Park Street Pulpit: Sermons of William Henry Harrison Murray.* Boston: James R. Osgood, 1871.

Nelson, Rudolph. *The Making and Unmaking of an Evangelical Mind.* Cambridge: Cambridge Univ. Press, 1987.

Noll, Mark A. *Between Faith and Criticism: Evangelicals, Scholarship, and the Bible.* San Francisco: Harper and Row, 1987.

———, David W. Bebbington, and George A. Rawlyk, eds. *Evangelicalism: Comparative Studies of Popular Protestantism in North America, the British*

Isles, and Beyond, 1700–1990. Religion in America Series. New York: Oxford Univ. Press, 1994.

———. *Jesus Christ and the Life of the Mind*. Grand Rapids: Eerdmans, 2011.

———. *The Scandal of the Evangelical Mind*. Grand Rapids: Eerdmans, 1994.

Nybakken, Elizabeth. "In the Irish Tradition: Pre-revolutionary Academies in America." *History of Education Quarterly* 37 (Summer 1997): 163–83.

Ockenga, Harold John. *The Church God Blesses*. Pasadena, Calif.: Fuller Missions Fellowship, 1959.

———. *The Church in God*. Westwood: Revell, 1956.

———. *The Comfort of God*. New York: Revell, 1944.

———. *The Epistles to the Thessalonians*. Grand Rapids: Baker, 1962.

———. *Every One That Believeth*. New York: Revell, 1942.

———. *Faith in a Troubled World*. Wenham, Mass.: Gordon College Press, 1972.

———. *Have You Met These Women?* Grand Rapids: Zondervan, 1940.

———. *Our Evangelical Faith*. Grand Rapids: Zondervan, 1946.

———. *Our Protestant Heritage*. Grand Rapids: Zondervan, 1938.

———. "Poverty as a Theoretical and Practical Problem of Government in the Writings of Jeremy Bentham and the Marxian Alternative." PhD diss., University of Pittsburgh, 1939.

———. *Power through Pentecost*. Grand Rapids: Eerdmans, 1959.

———. *Protestant Preaching through Lent*. Grand Rapids: Eerdmans, 1957.

———. *The Spirit of the Living God*. New York: Revell, 1947.

———. *These Religious Affections*. Grand Rapids: Zondervan, 1937.

———. *Women Who Made Bible History*. Grand Rapids: Zondervan, 1962.

Patterson, Bob E. *Carl F. H. Henry*. Makers of the Modern Theological Mind. Dallas: Word, 1984.

Phillips, John McCandless. "Protestants Map University Here." *New York Times*, May 5, 1960, A5.

Piper, John, and D. A. Carson. *The Pastor as Scholar and the Scholar as Pastor: Reflections on Life and Ministry*. Edited by Owen Strachan and David Mathis. Carol Stream, Ill.: Crossway, 2011.

Poling, Daniel. *Why Billy Graham?* Santa Fe, N.M.: Sunstone Press, 2008.

Porter, Daryl Alan. "*Christianity Today*: Its History and Development." ThM thesis, Dallas Theological Seminary, 1978.

Purdy, Richard A. "The Rational Apologetic Methodology of Carl F. H.

Henry in the Context of the Current Impasse between Reformed and Evangelical Apologetics." PhD diss., New York University, 1980.

Rice, John R. *I Am a Fundamentalist.* Murfreesboro, Tenn.: Sword of the Lord, 1975.

Rosas, Louis Joseph. "An Analysis of the Apologetic Method of Edward John Carnell." PhD diss., Southern Baptist Theological Seminary, 1980.

Rosell, Garth M. *Boston's Historic Park Street Church: The Story of an Evangelical Landmark.* Grand Rapids: Kregel, 2009.

———. *The Surprising Work of God: Harold John Ockenga, Billy Graham, and the Rebirth of Evangelicalism.* Grand Rapids: Baker, 2008.

Rust, Troy Neal. "The Preaching of Harold John Ockenga as a Response to the Perceived Excesses of Fundamentalism." PhD diss., Southern Baptist Theological Seminary, 2009.

Sandeen, Ernest Robert. *The Roots of Fundamentalism: British and American Millenarianism, 1800–1930.* Chicago: Univ. of Chicago Press, 1970.

Schultze, Quentin J., ed. *American Evangelicals and the Mass Media.* Grand Rapids: Zondervan, 1990.

Scott, Donald M. *From Office to Profession: The New England Ministry, 1750–1850.* Philadelphia: Univ. of Pennsylvania Press, 1978.

Sharp, Larry Dean. "Carl Henry: Neo-Evangelical Theologian." DMin thesis, Vanderbilt University, 1972.

Smith, David P. *B. B. Warfield's Scientifically Constructive Theological Scholarship.* The Evangelical Theological Society Monograph Series. Eugene, Ore.: Pickwick, 2011.

Snyder, Stephen. *Lyman Beecher and His Children: The Transformation of a Religious Tradition.* Chicago Studies in the History of American Religion. Brooklyn: Carlson, 1991.

Spittler, Russell, ed. *Fuller Voices: Then and Now.* Pasadena, Calif.: Fuller Seminary Press, 2004.

Stokes, David. *The Shooting Salvationist: J. Frank Norris and the Murder Trial That Captivated America.* New York: Random House, 2011.

Stonehouse, Ned. *J. Gresham Machen: A Biographical Memoir.* Grand Rapids: Eerdmans, 1954.

Strachan, Owen. "Carl Henry's Doctrine of the Atonement: A Synthesis and Brief Analysis." *Themelios* 38, no. 2 (Fall 2013): 215–31.

———. "Carl Henry's University Crusade: The Spectacular Promise and Ultimate Failure of Crusade University." *Trinity Journal* 35, no. 2 (Spring 2014): 25–44.

———. *Essential Evangelicalism: The Enduring Influence of Carl F. H. Henry.* Carol Stream, Ill.: Crossway, 2015.

———. "The Preacher Who Forged a New Evangelical Era: Harold Ockenga's Homiletical Approach to Theological History." *Theology for Ministry 3,* no. 2 (2008): 73–86.

Sutton, Matthew Avery. *Aimee Semple McPherson and the Resurrection of Christian America.* Cambridge: Harvard Univ. Press, 2007.

———. *American Apocalypse: A History of Modern Evangelicalism.* Cambridge: Harvard University Press, 2014.

Swartz, David. *Moral Minority: The Evangelical Left in an Age of Conservatism.* Philadelphia: Univ. of Pennsylvania Press, 2012.

Sweeney, Douglas A. *The American Evangelical Story: A History of the Movement.* Grand Rapids: Baker, 2005.

———. *Nathaniel Taylor, New Haven Theology, and the Legacy of Jonathan Edwards.* Religion in America Series. New York: Oxford Univ. Press, 2003.

Trollinger, William V. *God's Empire: William Bell Riley and Midwestern Fundamentalism.* Madison: Univ. of Wisconsin Press, 1991.

Turner, John G. *Bill Bright and Campus Crusade for Christ: The Renewal of Evangelicalism in Postwar America.* Chapel Hill: Univ. of North Carolina Press, 2008.

Utzinger, J. Michael. *Yet Saints Their Watch Are Keeping: Fundamentalists, Modernists, and the Development of Evangelical Ecclesiology, 1887–1937.* Macon, Ga.: Mercer Univ. Press, 2006.

Van Dusen, Henry. "Apostle to the Twentieth Century." *Atlantic Monthly,* 1934, 1–16.

Wacker, Grant. *America's Pastor: Billy Graham and the Shaping of a Nation.* Cambridge: Belknap, 2014.

———. "Billy Graham's America." *Church History* 78 (2009): 489–511.

———. *Heaven Below: Early Pentecostals and American Culture.* Cambridge: Harvard Univ. Press, 2001.

Ward, W. R. *Early Evangelicalism: A Global Intellectual History.* Cambridge: Cambridge Univ. Press, 2006.

White, Edward Charles. *The Beauty of Holiness: Phoebe Palmer as Theologian, Revivalist, Feminist, and Humanitarian.* Grand Rapids: Zondervan, 1986.

Wills, Gregory A. *The Southern Baptist Theological Seminary, 1859–2009.* New York: Oxford Univ. Press, 2009.

Woodridge, John D. *Biblical Authority: A Critique of the Rogers/McKim Proposal.* Grand Rapids: Zondervan, 1982.

——, **and Collin Hansen.** *A God-Sized Vision: Revival Stories That Strengthen and Stir.* Grand Rapids: Zondervan, 2010.

——, **and Thomas E. McComiskey, eds.** *Doing Theology in Today's World: Essays in Honor of Kenneth S. Kantzer.* Grand Rapids: Zondervan: 1994.

——, **and Wendy Murray Zoba.** "Standing on the Promises: Interview with Carl Henry and Kenneth Kantzer." *Christianity Today*, September 16, 1996, 28–35.

Worthen, Molly. *Apostles of Reason: The Crisis of Authority in American Evangelicalism.* New York: Oxford Univ. Press, 2013.

Young III, F. Lionel. "To the Right of Billy Graham: John R. Rice's 1957 Crusade against New Evangelicalism and the End of the Fundamentalist-Evangelical Coalition." ThM thesis, Trinity Evangelical Divinity School, 2005.

Youngs, William T. *God's Messengers: Religious Leadership in Colonial New England, 1700–1750.* Baltimore: Johns Hopkins Univ. Press, 1976.

Index